LITERATURE IN THE MODERN WORLD

BLOCK 7 LANGUAGE AND GENDER

Prepared for the course team by Dinah Birch, Cicely Palser Havely Michael Rossington and Dennis Walder

A 319

Arts: a third level course

The Open University

The course team

Richard Allen (author)
Jenny Bardwell (BBC producer)
Richard Bessel (author)
Dinah Birch (author)
Angus Calder (author)
Kate Clements (editor)
Tony Coe (BBC series producer and author)
Charles Cooper (BBC producer)
Tony Coulson (Library)
Abigail Croydon (editor)
Roger Day (author)
Andrew Ferguson (course manager)
Margaret Harvey (block rapporteur)
Cicely Palser Havely (author)
Pam Higgins (graphic designer)
G.D. Jayalakshmi (BBC producer)
Denis Johnson (tuition group chair)
Maggie Lawson (Project Control)
Beth Martin (BBC producer)
Graham Martin (course team chair, author)
Mags Noble (BBC producer)
W.R. Owens (editor of anthologies)
John Pettit (editor)
Michael Rossington (author)
Sue Staig (secretary)
Betty Talks (BBC producer)
Nora Tomlinson (tuition group)
Dennis Walder (author)
Keith Whitlock (author)
Amanda Willett (BBC producer)
Richard Wilson (block rapporteur)

Consultants

Dr Pamela Morris, member of the Open University's teaching and counselling staff (block assessor)
Professor Michael Wood, department of English literature at the University of Exeter (external assessor)

The Open University
Walton Hall, Milton Keynes MK7 6AA

First published 1991. Reprinted 1995, 1996, 1998

Typeset in 10 on 12 point Palatino.

Printed in the United Kingdom by Page Bros, Norwich

ISBN 0 7492 1041 9

This block is part of an Open University course. The complete list of blocks is given at the end of this binding.

If you have not enrolled on the course and would like to buy this or other Open University material, please write to Open University Educational Enterprises Limited, 12 Cofferidge Close, Stony Stratford, Milton Keynes, MK11 1BY, United Kingdom.

If you wish to enquire about enrolling as an Open University student, please write to: The Admissions Office, The Open University, PO Box 48, Walton Hall, Milton Keynes MK7 6AB, United Kingdom.

1.4

2308C/A319b6i1.4

Contents

(Dinah Birch wrote Sections 1, 3, 4, 6, 7 and 10–12; Cicely Palser Havely wrote Sections 2 and 5; Michael Rossington wrote Section 9 and Dennis Walder wrote Section 8)

Required reading

D.H. Lawrence (1970) *The Virgin and the Gipsy*, Penguin, first published 1930 (set book)

Virginia Woolf, 'Kew Gardens' (in the Prose Anthology)

Ernest Hemingway, 'The Short Happy Life of Francis Macomber' (in the Prose Anthology)

Stevie Smith, poems (in the Poetry Anthology)

Stevie Smith, extract from *Over the Frontier* (in the Prose Anthology)

Sylvia Plath, poems (in the Poetry Anthology)

Elizabeth Bishop, 'In the Village' (in the Prose Anthology)

Elizabeth Bishop, poems (in the Poetry Anthology)

Adrienne Rich, poem (in the Poetry Anthology)

Toni Morrison (1989) *Song of Solomon*, Picador, first published 1977 (set book)

From the A319 Reader

Simone de Beauvoir, 'Woman and the Other'

Virginia Woolf, 'To Cambridge women'

Sandra Gilbert and Susan Gubar, 'Women poets'

Cora Kaplan, 'Language and gender'

Hélène Cixous, 'The laugh of the Medusa'

Toni Morrison, 'Rootedness: the ancestor as foundation'

(The A319 Reader is *Literature in the Modern World*, edited by Dennis Walder, 1990, Oxford University Press/The Open University.)

Broadcasts/cassettes

TV13 *The Gentle Sex? Representations of Gender* (linked to Section 1)

TV14 *Changing Voices* (Section 6)

Radio 13 *Masculine Women, Feminine Men: D.H. Lawrence* (Section 2)

Radio 14 *Feminist Debates: Psychoanalysis* (Section 3)

Audio-cassette 4 Side 1, 'Stevie Smith' (Section 7)

(See also the Broadcast and Cassette Notes.)

Aims and objectives

The purpose of this block is to further your understanding of how literature in the modern world intersects with the issues of language and gender. It won't be possible to think about every aspect of the subject – it's too huge. We shall concentrate on two principal aims:

(a) to outline how language in its relation to gender came to be recognized as a matter of central concern to those interested in literature, as writers and as readers. To do this, we will look at the history and development of the most significant strands in feminist theory, for it is through the work of feminism that the issues have come to critical prominence;

(b) to develop your understanding of a diversity of texts, by both men and women, in the light of what feminist theories have proposed as important issues.

1 Introduction

Why feminist theory?

1.1 This is not the first time you have been asked to think about the impact of gender on literature. The issues were introduced in general terms in Block 1 Section 4, and in the context of Virginia Woolf's fiction in Block 2 Section 4. Gender, you will remember, is defined in those sections as the *cultural construction* of concepts of femininity and masculinity, as distinct from the biological sex – male or female – we are all born with. Throughout succeeding blocks of the course, you have encountered texts that reflect the complex polarities of language and gender. The fiction of Graham Greene or R.K. Narayan, the poetry of T.S. Eliot or Grace Nichols and the drama of Beckett or Lorca – all these can be used to demonstrate ways in which writers, readers, audiences and critics have reacted to the various ideologies we have attached to notions of the feminine and the masculine. So far, however, you haven't had a chance to develop a theoretical framework in which to place your response to these diverse texts. And you may well see little need to do so. Why not simply concentrate on the texts?

1.2 If you find yourself asking this question, you have identified an argument that is central to the debates we shall be pursuing. A new and sometimes sceptical exploration of the kind of thinking that we term 'theoretical' has been one of the results of looking at language and gender in literature. Before proceeding any further, we need to consider the grounds for this scepticism.

1.3 Most, though not all, of those who have been interested in the ways in which language and gender define each other have been feminists. Feminism is a term that includes a host of positions, some much more radical than others. For our purposes here, it's enough to say that feminists are those who wish to expose and to challenge women's cultural and political disadvantage. If you turn back to your notes on the introductory sections on language and gender in Block 1 Section 4 and Block 2 Section 4, you will recall that one of the suppositions that feminists have drawn attention to is the idea that formal, abstract thought, which has the power to draw general principles from detail and particularity, is naturally the domain of the male mind, and that such abstract discourse is to be given a higher status than a more personal or emotional language, which is supposedly the province of the female. There are two ways of attacking this assumption. Firstly, it might be argued that the notion that a girl is born with a feebler capacity for theoretical logic than her brother is fundamentally misogynist and mistaken. Feminists taking this line would therefore claim equal access to these patriarchal territories, asserting women's right to the formulation of theory. But it is also possible to adopt a second line of argument and say that the problem lies not so much in the exclusion of women from abstract language, as in the low value that has been set on the different kinds of discourse that women have made, or might make, their own.

1.4 These two lines of approach are not mutually exclusive. But most feminists have tended to favour either one or the other. Those who tend towards the second position distrust the wish to compete with the voices of patriarchy. They have often preferred to try to develop their own varieties of language. This is clearly true of those feminist dramatists, poets or novelists who have remodelled literary traditions according to their own imaginative needs. But it is also true of feminist critics, who often refuse to draw a line between critical and creative work. Virginia Woolf is an influential example of this tendency, for there is no fixed distinction between her fiction and her social and literary criticism. As we shall see in looking at the more recent writings of Adrienne Rich (whose work fuses poetry and criticism) or Hélène Cixous (a playwright and novelist as well as critic), it isn't always easy to classify feminist work.

1.5 You may already have noticed this for yourself, if you have read any quantity of feminist criticism, literary or of any other kind. Feminist academics will often adopt, as a matter of deliberate strategy, a more personal or autobiographical approach than is usual within the traditions of scholarly discourse, which aim at detachment and objectivity. In this sense, the shared purposes of feminist theorists and feminist writers – to explore and perhaps to create a language for women – mean that the two central aims of this block (see p.5) are not separate.

1.6 But such thinking has its dangers. To be personal is to invite dismissal as an emotional – or worse still, chatty – woman. Feminists working in academic institutions commonly insist that the women's movement must be prepared to present a coherent and sophisticated theoretical justification of its aims in order to confront its solidly established adversaries effectively. Practising writers often put forward another view, claiming that the wish to rewrite or remodel literary language is simply irrelevant, for language is genderless. For those who think that way, the aim of feminism in literature (if it has any business there at all) is to ensure an equality of treatment. Such arguments have often been adopted by those reluctant to see themselves labelled, and perhaps dismissed, as *women* writers rather than just writers. Stevie Smith felt like this, as we shall see, and the poet Elizabeth Jennings expresses a similar position in TV14 (*Changing Voices*). Jennings has no wish to identify a feminine voice, only to see her work received on equal terms with that of men.

1.7 These are by no means the only points of controversy we shall encounter, for argument is the lifeblood of feminist thinking. The disputes have primarily been with inheritors of that masculine privilege which the movement seeks to examine and undermine. But feminists are also quite ready to argue with each other. For those not acquainted with the terms of the debates, this combination of self-awareness and combativeness can be daunting. Feminists are united by some fundamental beliefs and objectives and their work often assumes that their readers will at least know about, if they do not share, these convictions. The advantage of looking at the roots of feminist thought is that it leads to an understanding of what its leading proponents disagree about – and, perhaps more importantly, what they do not disagree about. Such an understanding will lead us to read both literature and criticism with new kinds of awareness.

Virginia Woolf and women's history

1.8 Your work on Virginia Woolf for Block 2 focused on *Mrs Dalloway*. But you also encountered a non-fictional text by Woolf which is now regarded as one of the most significant starting points in the history of modern feminism. Woolf's *A Room of One's Own* is only secondarily a work of literary criticism. Now itself a part of history, the book invites us to open our eyes to what we mean by history, to examine how our images of the past are produced.

ACTIVITY

In *A Room of One's Own*, Woolf thinks about the Elizabethan age, traditionally esteemed as the most luminous in English literature. How did women figure in what were, in 1928, the most prestigious histories of the period? Read the following passage, which is not in your Reader extract, and make notes on what strike you as the most significant points in Woolf's argument:

> Occasionally an individual woman is mentioned, an Elizabeth, or a Mary; a queen or a great lady. But by no possible means could middle-class women with nothing but brains or character at their command have taken part in any one of the great movements which, brought together, constitute the historian's view of the past. Nor shall we find her in any collection of anecdotes ... Aubrey hardly mentions her. She never writes her own life and scarcely keeps a diary; there are only a handful of her letters in existence. She left no plays or poems by which we can judge her. What one wants, I thought – and why does not some brilliant student at Newnham or Girton supply it? – is a mass of information; at what age did she marry; how many children had she as a rule; what was her house like, and had she a room to herself; did she do the cooking; would she be likely to have a servant? All these facts lie somewhere, presumably, in parish registers and account books; the life of the average Elizabethan woman must be scattered about somewhere, could one collect it and make a book of it. It would be ambitious beyond my daring, I thought, looking about the shelves for books that were not there, to suggest to the students of those famous colleges that they should rewrite history, though I own that it often seems a little queer as it is, unreal, lop-sided; but why should they not add a supplement to history, calling it, of course, by some inconspicuous name so that women might figure there without impropriety? For one often catches a glimpse of them in the lives of the great, whisking away into the background, concealing, I sometimes think, a wink, a laugh, perhaps a tear.
>
> (Woolf, 1977, pp.44–5; the reference is to John Aubrey, 1626–97, famous for his *Lives of eminent men.*)

DISCUSSION

Woolf's basic point seems to me a simple one, forcefully and persuasively expressed. Conventional histories have simply ignored women. A new kind of history, based on research undertaken by a new breed of academic woman, is called for: history that would disinter the forgotten lives of women buried in history.

A Room of One's Own was first published in 1929; as we have noted, it has itself become a part of history, bearing the visible marks of Woolf's own cultural situation. What, for instance, did you make of the sleight of hand that leads Woolf silently to equate 'middle-class women' with 'the *average* Elizabethan woman' – very few of whom could read? It is clear enough that this average woman was not middle-class; equally clear that standard histories of the kind Woolf has in mind have excluded the experience of the poor quite as ruthlessly as they have disregarded women. For all her lucid scrutiny of the iniquities of a patriarchal society, Woolf was never quite able to enter imaginatively into the experiences of those outside the bounds of her own privileged social class. Woolf is not much interested in what the life of the servant possibly employed by the middle-class woman might have been like. The limits of her perspective are reflected in her language: the pronoun 'one' – used three times in this passage (and of course, not coincidentally, part of the title of Woolf's book) – was then, as now, a mark of middle-class discourse. Nevertheless, the gist of Woolf's message, with its anger, scarcely veiled by the coolly ironic tone ('calling it, of course, by some inconspicuous name so that women might figure there without impropriety...'), is firm enough. Though Woolf was not to be alone in noting the neglect of women by professional historians, few made the observation with quite such incisive effect.

1.9 Despite her interest in the complexities of the inner life, there was a very hard-headed and businesslike side to Woolf's mind. In *A Room of One's Own,* she points to the solid economic obstacles that blocked the aspirations of the talented women of the past. Her central point is that writing was (and is) impossible without a certain degree of economic independence. Women lacked education, freedom and the means to publish their work. They rarely had rooms of their own. Their role in literature had been a substantial one, but it had largely been confined to acting as vehicles for the preoccupations of male authors:

> Some of the most inspired words, some of the most profound thoughts in literature fall from her lips; in real life she could hardly read, could scarcely spell, and was the property of her husband.
>
> (Ibid., p.43)

The question of false representations of women in literature, and particularly in fiction, was one that became important to those who went on to develop the ideas outlined in Woolf's cutting polemic. The origins and growth of recurrent stereotypes – the witch, the virgin, the whore, the spinster, to name some of the most familiar – received concentrated attention, particularly in North American universities, in the late sixties and early seventies, and the ubiquity of such images of women is now commonly accepted as a feature of literary history.

1.10 But the study of such images, or their condemnation, has not been the only concern of the feminist literary scholarship that came after Woolf. More than sixty years after she wrote, the history of women in literature – as figures in books, writers of books, or as readers – is not nearly such a dark and untraversed field as it was when she wrote *A Room of One's Own*. The challenge that Woolf threw down was eagerly taken up by many students – not all of them, it should be said, from Newnham or Girton, those illustrious Cambridge colleges for women which, in the 1920s, drew their students exclusively from the middle classes. Some of the books that Woolf sought in vain have now been written. They have not always taken quite the forms that she envisaged, but they have, as she hoped, set out to find a voice for matters that had been passed over in silence for too long. Some of these questions are explored in TV13 *The Gentle Sex? Representations of gender*. How did the business of recording history come to be such a masculine pursuit? Why have most poets been men? Why have most dramatists been men? How has it happened that even in terms of the genre in which women have traditionally been admitted to excel – the novel – masculine values and reputations can be seen to dominate? Many of the answers to such questions have turned out to be grounded, as Woolf foreshadowed, in the hard facts of women's long economic subjugation. Revealing the extent of that subjugation has not been the least consequential of the achievements of feminists after Woolf. As a general rule, poor and uneducated people do not write books, still less publish them, whether they are women or men. Women have been, and are still, more likely to be poor and uneducated then men. Small wonder, then, that they have written fewer books.

1.11 But that is clearly not the end of the matter, though it is an important beginning. Women have written fewer books than men. Nevertheless they have, often in the face of considerable difficulty, written books. One of the most influential currents of development in feminist criticism has been directed towards a detailed examination of the neglected tradition of women's writing. Forgotten female authors have been reinstated; the work of more established figures has been re-examined. American critics have been the spearhead of this movement: books such as Ellen Moer's *Literary Women* (1976), Elaine Showalter's *A Literature of Their Own* (1977), or Sandra Gilbert and Susan Gubar's *The Madwoman in the Attic* (1979) are major works of their kind. With different emphases and perspectives, they concentrate on what had been written *out* of previous constructions of literary history. These books discover, document and analyse what women have accomplished in literature.

For students in the seventies, they made exhilarating reading, and their impact has proved to be lasting.

1.12 These North American critics have asserted that what Woolf noticed in 1928 remains pervasively true, in ways that Woolf did not explore. Women persistently vanish from the historical record. Elaine Showalter, a critic who has been one of the strongest voices in American feminist literary criticism for many years, was one of the first to document the melancholy phenomenon of the disappearing woman. Even those women who were famous in their own lifetimes are effaced from the records of posterity, therefore 'each generation of women writers has found itself, in a sense, without a history, forced to rediscover the past anew, forging again and again the consciousness of their sex'. American feminists have been concerned with the rediscovery of lost women, lost female resistance, lost achievement. Their project has accordingly been dedicated to filling in the gaps and the silences in our patriarchal discourses on the past. Adrienne Rich states the case forcefully in her book *On Lies, Secrets and Silence*:

> The entire history of women's struggle for self-determination has been muffled in silence over and over. One serious cultural obstacle encountered by any feminist writer is that each feminist work has tended to be received as if it emerged from nowhere; as if each of us had lived, thought and worked without any historical past or contextual present. This is one of the ways in which women's work and women's thinking has been made to seem sporadic, errant, orphaned of any tradition of its own.
>
> In fact, we do have a long feminist tradition both oral and written, a tradition which has built on itself over and over, recovering essential elements even when those have been strangled or wiped out. Yet still a Mary Wollstonecraft (labelled 'the hyena in petticoats') is viewed without reference to her forebears, not only the sixteenth-century women pamphleteers, but the wisewomen and witches, who had been the objects of wholesale persecution and massacre for three centuries. So also Simone de Beauvoir has been read without reference to the destruction of the political women's clubs of the French Revolution, or the writings of Olympe de Gouges and Flora Tristan. So also has the articulate political feminism of Virginia Woolf been obscured by the notion that she was 'Bloomsbury' – individualist, elitist, lacking class-consciousness, and 'gay' in the most frivolous sense, without reference to her connections with Margaret Llewelyn Davies, the Women's Cooperative Guild, the antipatriarchal anthropologist Jane Harrison, the lesbian/feminist suffrage activist Ethel Smyth. So also is each contemporary feminist theorist attacked or dismissed *ad feminam*[1] , as if her politics were simply an outburst of personal bitterness or rage.
>
> (1979, pp.11–12)

Note: Mary Wollstonecraft's important *A Vindication of the Rights of Woman*, influenced by the events of the French Revolution, was published in 1792. In the same year, Olympe de Gouges dedicated her *Déclaration des droits de la femme et de la citoyen* ('Declaration of the rights of woman and of the citizen') to the queen. De Gouges was executed in 1793. Flora Tristan published her feminist and socialist *Union ouvrière* ('Workers' union') in 1843. Margaret Llewelyn Davies shared many of Woolf's feminist views. Jane Harrison held the first research fellowship at Newnham College. One of the founders of modern anthropology, she played a central role in establishing the importance of ritual in the history of mythology and religion. Ethel Smyth was a distinguished musician as well as an active campaigner for voting rights for women.

1.13 Writing of this kind has been profoundly influential. Women have been given the sense that they are not alone, that they have a history that matters. Others have been here before.

[1]*ad feminam*: (usually in the masculine, *ad hominem*) – on personal grounds.

Simone de Beauvoir's *The Second Sex*

1.14 Adrienne Rich is North American, and one of her first concerns as an active feminist is to retrace the outlines of a long tradition of feminist thought in the US. In the passage we have just looked at, however, she cites the feminist history of Europe. One of the women she mentions, Simone de Beauvoir (1908–86), has, like Virginia Woolf, now established herself as a dominant figure in the history of feminist thought. The text that gives her this status, *The Second Sex* (first published in 1949), is a work of a very different kind from Woolf's *A Room of One's Own*. You don't even have to read the books to register the first and most obvious difference. For all its cogency, *A Room of One's Own* is a very slim volume. Its origins lie in two lectures that Woolf delivered in Cambridge in October 1928, and though she later revised and expanded what she had said, the book does not pretend to be a major work of scholarship. De Beauvoir's ambitions in writing *The Second Sex* were on another scale altogether. Her book is in every sense a massive work. It was her intention to show that what had been circumscribed as 'the woman question' had implications of a kind that had never been realized, or expressed: it lay at the heart of any form of human culture. It followed, then, that all intellectual domains and disciplines were not merely relevant, but essential, to an understanding of what cultural projections of femininity implied. Anthropology and history, literary criticism and biology, psychoanalysis, political science, autobiography, sociology, philosophy – all are included in de Beauvoir's monumental analysis of what it means to be a woman. De Beauvoir was not rejecting the points made twenty years previously by Woolf; she acknowledges Woolf, among others, and she too takes as an indispensable starting-point the fact of women's economic dependence. She also emphasizes that 'in the past all history has been made by men' (1977 edition, p.21). But de Beauvoir was in a position to go far beyond anything that Woolf had attempted.

1.15 'One is not born, but rather becomes, a woman' (ibid., p.295). De Beauvoir began the second volume of her work with what has become the most famous single sentence in the history of feminist criticism. The point is a simple one, though its consequences are not. There is, de Beauvoir insists, no such thing as a female nature, made up of essentially female qualities. Concepts of femininity are socially constructed, not biologically determined. The purpose of de Beauvoir's argument is to show how the subordination of women has become a universal phenomenon. She was accordingly less concerned with particular cultural or historical contexts of patriarchal ideology than with the fact of its global dominance. Its impositions are so deeply embedded in our experience that it calls for the most wide-ranging intellectual analysis to recognize and study its origins and growth. Once exposed, its power might, de Beauvoir argued, be challenged. But that would involve change of a kind so far-reaching that it could never take place in isolation. When De Beauvoir sat down to write *The Second Sex*, she did not see herself as a feminist. She was a socialist, committed to the view that women's oppression would only end with socialist revolution, and that her work towards that revolution must always take priority over her work for women.

1.16 She was to change her mind. In 1972, she joined the *Mouvement de Libération des Femmes* (MLF – the French women's liberation movement), and made her first public commitment to active feminism. Her action arose from years of disillusionment:

> At the end of *The Second Sex*, I said I wasn't a feminist because I thought that the solution to women's problems must depend on the socialist evolution of society. By feminist, I meant fighting for specifically feminine demands independent of the class struggle. Today my definition is the

> same, but I have come to realize that we must fight for an improvement in women's actual situation before achieving the socialism we hope for. Besides this, I realized that even in the socialist countries, women's equality has not been won. So it is necessary for women to fight for their rights. That is why I have now joined the MLF.
>
> Another reason is that even in the French leftist movements, there is serious inequality between men and women. Women always do the humblest, most boring, and least visible jobs. The men speak, write articles, do the most interesting things, and have the greatest responsibilities. In the bosom of these movements, in principle formed to liberate everybody – including youth and women – women remain inferior.
>
> It goes even further. Many male leftists are aggressively hostile to women's liberation. They despise us and let us know it. The first time a feminist meeting was held in Vincennes, a number of male leftists broke into the hall shouting 'Power to the phallus!'. I think they are beginning to revise that position, just because women are demonstrating that they can conduct a militant action independent of men.
>
> (quoted in Marks and de Courtivron, 1981, pp.143–4)

De Beauvoir's sobering experience as a socialist woman was not unique; nor was her conversion. During the 1970s, socialism in France gave rise to a distinct and energetic feminist movement, with philosophical and political roots significantly different, though not wholly separate, from the foundations of the feminism that was developing during this period in North America or elsewhere in Europe.

1.17 It is often a philosophical rather than political orientation that forms the organizing principle of de Beauvoir's immense essay. She met Jean-Paul Sartre as a student at the Sorbonne and formed a close relationship with him which lasted until his death in 1980. Sartre was a central figure in the existentialist movement in France and, in the 1940s, de Beauvoir's thinking was deeply influenced by his philosophy. Existentialism was never a formally constituted school of philosophy; nor was it always a very consistent one. The important point to register here is that existentialist thought tends to emphasize the pre-eminence of the experience of the individual as a measure of human stature. What is unique in our lives is given precedence over the common values of shared progress or profit. From this starting-point follows the belief that we must take responsibility for our own separate destinies. God has no hand in our spiritual fate, for he does not, Sartre argues, exist. We must make our own moral choices. To allow any other person – or culture, or faith – to make them for us is to deny the full measure of our humanity. From moments of pure decision proceed the features of our characters and our ambitions. But in order to make such decisions, we must live without illusion: an authentic sense of self must rest on a full realization of the unalterable facts of human life, human suffering, and especially human mortality.

1.18 Such an emphasis on the inescapable need for each individual to take charge of her or his own moral destiny must have seemed timely after the events of Hitler's war in Europe. The career of Nazism had provided a grim illustration of what the results of renouncing that responsibility might be. It's clear, too, that the tenets of existentialism might well be of interest to a novelist, for the novel had traditionally been concerned with the formation of character, and with the moral consequences of character in action. It's no accident that Sartre, Camus and de Beauvoir, each with a close creative relationship with existential thinking, were novelists of great distinction, with a keen interest in the moral and philosophical potential they discerned in the traditions of fiction. Camus's *The Outsider*, with its relentless concentration on Meursault as a solitary individual choosing a bleak but authentic destiny, is very much a case in point. But it may not be so clear how de Beauvoir's existential values modified the terms of her analysis of culturally constructed femininity.

ACTIVITY

In order to try to trace some of the connections, I want to look at the extracts from the introduction to *The Second Sex* which you will find reprinted in your Reader ('Woman and the Other', pp.305–10). Could you now turn to these extracts?

When you have read the extracts, make notes summarizing what seem to you to be the most important points in de Beauvoir's argument. You might find it useful to concentrate on the following questions:

(a) What seem to you the basic grounds of de Beauvoir's dissatisfaction with the definitions of woman that she describes?

(b) Do you see any points of contact between her position and the kind of existential thought exemplified by Sartre and Camus?

DISCUSSION

(a) De Beauvoir's fundamental argument seems to come down to one central statement: women have, for long centuries, been regarded as the 'Other'; man is the 'absolute human type', woman is 'the incidental, the inessential'. Woman is simply everything that man is not. He is positive, she is negative. Men, who have claimed the right of definition for themselves, have persistently seen women only in relation to their own situation, rather than as autonomous beings in their own right. The result has been that women have been denied the essential privilege of subjectivity. They have, often willingly, found themselves in a position where they are not permitted to answer for their moral destiny. They have been reduced, in effect, to objects.

(b) Clearly, the condition that de Beauvoir describes is one that robs women of what existential thought would regard as the most basic qualification for human worth. As individuals (and de Beauvoir reminds us of the existential conviction that it is finally the individual who matters), they are not likely to find the means to transcend their immanence, or 'stagnation'. They are denied (or deny themselves, with a complicity that de Beauvoir has no hesitation in terming 'a moral fault') freedom of choice. In de Beauvoir's terms, which are here close to those of existential philosophy, the function as the 'Other' that men have imposed on women deny them the chance to achieve full membership of the human race.

1.19 De Beauvoir's closely reasoned exposure of the baleful effects of women's cultural confinement as the 'Other' had comprehensive implications. One of the most seductive aspects of her argument, from the point of view of the women who read her book, was the idea that the social role of women, like any other role, finally came down to a matter of choice. The assumption was that, once armed with the 'clarity and understanding' provided by the kind of analysis that de Beauvoir had undertaken, women would simply choose not to be confined by the terms inflicted on them by men. They would opt to be free. De Beauvoir's own life as a distinguished intellectual – unmarried, childless, sitting in bohemian cafés rather than doing the washing-up, claiming her entitlement to be regarded as fully the equal of her male associates – seemed a glamorous vindication of the possibility, even the ease, of such choices. To many who came after her, and finally to de Beauvoir herself, the notion that women as individuals could simply choose liberty came to seem naïve. But the glimpse of freedom offered in *The Second Sex* was an intoxicating one, no matter how illusory it turned out to be. It has not been forgotten. De Beauvoir has permanently changed the way in which women see themselves.

De Beauvoir and D.H. Lawrence

1.20 *The Second Sex* is not primarily a work of literary criticism. But de Beauvoir was a novelist before she embarked on her feminist scholarship and her book reflects her preoccupation with fiction in many ways. Like *A Room of One's Own*, *The Second Sex* incorporates narrative strategy into argument. De Beauvoir makes free use of constructed reminiscence to support and extend her analysis, often, like Woolf, writing out of her own experience. Suspicious of objective impartiality, she claims the creative freedom to write with a lyrical and rhythmic drive that is capable of expressing the intensity of her commitment. Unhappily, not all of these qualities are evident in the standard English translation of the work. Howard Parshley, who published his translation in 1953, was a professor of zoology in Massachusetts. It was a large undertaking and de Beauvoir's many English-speaking readers owe him a debt of gratitude. But literary refinement cannot be counted among Parshley's virtues, and the English book he produced is sometimes spectacularly laboured and pompous. More worrying, perhaps, as feminist scholars have pointed out, are the grounds on which he has deleted ten per cent of the French text. As translated by a man, *The Second Sex* has a good deal less to say about the dreariness of housework than de Beauvoir intended. Not all of de Beauvoir's literary criticism escapes Parshley's secateurs. Her treatment of lesbian poetry, for instance, vanishes. But what she has to say about fiction remains in Parshley's translation as a prominent feature of her argument. De Beauvoir is primarily interested in what men have made of women, rather than what women have made of themselves. She focuses, therefore, on the exploration of fictions by men rather than the discovery of writing by women. Though she does cite women writers as sources of experiential evidence, she reserves her most detailed analysis for the work of four Frenchmen (Henri de Montherlant, Paul Claudel, André Breton, and Stendhal), and one Englishman – D.H. Lawrence.

1.21 Of these writers, only Stendhal earns de Beauvoir's praise, on the grounds that he is prepared to describe women as they are, rather than investing them with the specious spiritual mystery projected by the male ego. Her objections to the other four authors arise from her existentialist interpretation of the ways in which fictional women, like their flesh and blood counterparts, have been required to conform to the role of the 'Other'. Lawrence might initially seem an honourable exception, for he is sceptical of some of the traditional norms of masculinity, and apparently celebrates an equality between the sexes. De Beauvoir comments that, in Lawrence, 'She [woman] is just as real as the man, and a real communion is what he should achieve' (op. cit., p.248). But this equality is, she argues, an illusion; in fact Lawrence 'believes passionately in the supremacy of the male' (p.248). De Beauvoir translates Lawrence's mystical idealization of the 'phallic marriage', sardonically and at length, into her own socialist and existentialist terms. In his insistence that woman should subordinate her existence to that of man, Lawrence reveals himself to be, at heart, a traditional bourgeois. Only through the mediation of the transcendent man can woman, in Lawrence's fictive world, realize her identity. De Beauvoir comments:

> We can see why Lawrence's novels are, above all, 'guidebooks for women'. It is much more difficult for woman than for man to 'accept the universe', for man submits to the cosmic order autonomously, whereas woman needs the mediation of the male. There is really a surrender when for woman the Other takes the shape of an alien consciousness and will; on the contrary, an

> autonomous submission, as by man, remarkably resembles a sovereign decision. Either the heroes of Lawrence are condemned at the start, or from the start they hold the secret of wisdom; their submission to the cosmos has been accomplished so long since, and they derive from it so much inner certainty, that they seem as arrogant as any proud individualist; there is a god who speaks through them: Lawrence himself. As for woman, it is for her to bow down before their divinity. In so far as man is a phallus and not a brain, the individual who has his share of virility keeps his advantages; woman is not evil, she is even good – but subordinated. It is once more the ideal of the 'true woman' that Lawrence has to offer us – that is, the woman who unreservedly accepts being defined as the Other.
>
> (Op. cit., pp.253–4)

It should be said that this is an example of Parshley's translation at its most graceless. Nevertheless, de Beauvoir's point emerges clearly enough. Lawrence's vision of the ideal relationship between the sexes is one that excludes woman from her most basic right to self-determination.

1.22 De Beauvoir does not offer a complete reading of Lawrence. Nor, in terms of contemporary narratological theory, does she offer a sophisticated one. Like many early feminist critics of the novel, she is very ready to assume a straightforward identity between the views of the novelist and the views of his characters. She has a particular point of view to proclaim, and she makes the novels a good deal simpler than they might now appear. She was, nevertheless, attempting something quite original. The substantial work that has since been done to reveal the fictional subordination of women makes it easy for us to underestimate this originality. Such criticism has become familiar. But no one had written like that about Lawrence, or about any other novelist, in 1949. De Beauvoir's radical scepticism as a feminist literary critic was to have lasting consequences.

Kate Millett's *Sexual Politics*

1.23 The influence of de Beauvoir's innovatory study has made itself felt in a broad range of feminist thinking. But twenty years were to pass before a work of literary criticism appeared that had an impact that could be described as comparable with de Beauvoir's. Kate Millett's extraordinary *Sexual Politics* (first published in 1969) is an academic classic, but one with a popular appeal that made it more than a work of scholarship. Its origins lay in a Ph.D thesis, but it became a best-selling blockbuster. This is the book that really put feminist criticism on the map.

1.24 It could not have been written without *The Second Sex* – though Millett was inclined to make the most of her status as hard-hitting pioneer, and her acknowledgements of the predecessors from whom she learnt most, including de Beauvoir, were scant. Like de Beauvoir, Millett looks at fiction as both an expression and a cause of the subordination of women. Marxists had pointed to a relationship between the classes based on domination and exploitation. Now feminists could show a relationship between the sexes that was equally political in this fundamental sense, equally based on manipulation and rule. Millett showed how the language of power inscribed itself deeply on texts with a privileged status as the vehicles of high culture.

1.25 The fiction of D.H. Lawrence was, for Millett as for de Beauvoir, a test case. Like de Beauvoir, Millett has a point to make – in her case, a bluntly political rather than a philosophical point. In Millett's interpretation, Lawrence's women represent the enemy rather than the 'Other'. Millett argues that Lawrence felt alarmed and threatened by the processes that were beginning to liberate women's lives in the early twentieth century. If woman, with her ability to give birth and sustain life, should also prove capable of earning her own living in the public world, then what was left for man?

> He is bettered in his own field and beaten in hers. Most of Lawrence's sexual politics appears to spring from this vision of the emancipation of women; many of the preoccupations of his later work are a response to it.
>
> (1977, p.260)

Seen in these terms, Lawrence's fiction can be interpreted as a concerted attempt to put women back into their proper place – as the servants and supports of their men. He emerges from Millett's analysis as a self-serving reactionary, not a radical. Millett takes *Lady Chatterley's Lover*, Lawrence's tale of passion between an aristocratic woman and her husband's gamekeeper, among her examples:

> The lovers have not so much bridged class as transcended it into an aristocracy presumably based on sexual dynamism rather than on wealth or position. The very obnoxious Lord [sic!] Chatterley represents the insufferable white male of the master caste, pretending to be worthy of the term 'ruling class'. Mellors and Lawrence are born outsiders to the privileged white man's general sway of empire, mine ownership, and the many other privileges of a male élite. But this has not persuaded them to overthrow so much as to envy, imitate, and covet. Rather in the manner of a black who is so corroded with white values that his grandest aspiration is sexual acceptance by the white woman, Lawrence's dark outsiders, whether Mexican Indian or Derbyshire collier, focus their attention on the 'white man's woman' – the Lady. Women of his own class and kind are beneath his contempt...
>
> (Ibid., p.244)

A generation of predominantly female English-speaking students of literature had been taught by F.R. Leavis and his followers (Leavis's celebratory *D.H. Lawrence: novelist* came out in 1955) to revere Lawrence as one of the greatest English novelists of the twentieth century. Not all of them read de Beauvoir, but many read Millett, and Millett changed everything. Such was the effect of Millett's barbed prose, substantiated with extensive and shrewdly chosen quotation from the novels, that Lawrence came to seem, in the eyes of many, not only sinister and vicious but – more damaging still – ridiculous. Millett had a knack of making the most towering male pretension look like a farcical joke – one of the main reasons for her popularity among female students. But she was only able to do so by excluding those aspects of her chosen targets that did not support her overall view. Hilary Simpson re-examines these issues from new perspectives in the radio programme associated with Section 2 of this block (Radio 13 *Masculine Women, Feminine Men: D.H. Lawrence*). Millett's view of Lawrence was neither complete nor final. What does she leave out? This is a question to keep in mind in your reading of *The Virgin and the Gypsy* – another story of a lady and a dark outsider.

2 D.H. Lawrence: 'The Virgin and the Gypsy'

2.1 *The Virgin and the Gypsy* was composed in 1925–6 though not published till 1930; thus it is one of Lawrence's later works, although its North of England setting and its family themes revert to some of the characteristics of much earlier work. It was written in Italy, at the onset of what was to be his long final illness.

2.2 Throughout, a cool, austere landscape, beautifully remembered, forms a background in contrast to the fetid, suffocating atmosphere of a middle-class household. The rectory represents all that Lawrence had come to hate in England. Returning briefly a couple of years after writing this story he wrote:

> The traffic of London used to roar with the mystery of man's adventures in the seas of life, like a vast sea-shell, murmuring a thrilling, half-comprehensible story. Now it booms like monotonous, far-off guns, in a monotony of crushing something, crushing the earth, crushing out life, crushing everything dead.
>
> (*Evening News*, 3 September 1928)

ACTIVITY

Though the war had been over for ten years, those 'far-off guns' seem to suggest a conflict unresolved and perhaps in need of finishing. As you read *The Virgin and the Gypsy* – which you should do now – ask yourself whether Lawrence believed that the house of England needed to be destroyed in some second Flood, and whether, at another level, the cleansing waters represent a need to sweep away the old, stifling attitudes to sex.

Gender and Lawrence's prose

2.3 Do men and women speak and write a different language? In *A Room of One's Own* Virginia Woolf maintained that a woman novelist in the nineteenth century would have found 'that there was no common sentence ready for her use'. Look back to Block 2 Section 4 where this issue was first raised. Woolf is hard to pin down here. Though she invents an example of 'a man's sentence', she refuses to tell us exactly where Charlotte Brontë 'stumbled'. The gendering of language is a subject that will be debated again in later sections, but before then it will be useful to put together some relatively untheorized thoughts on the subject in relation to this story.

ACTIVITY

Re-read a few pages of *The Virgin and the Gypsy* and ask yourself whether its language characteristically has much in common with Woolf's idea of a 'man's sentence'.

DISCUSSION

I think you will have noticed that Lawrence's style is very idiosyncratic, and I want to suggest that when we try to gender its characteristics they seem to be distinctly 'feminine'. His language certainly resists those standards of correctness usually associated with authority or patriarchy. His sentences are unstructured, loosely organized and informal; they are emphatic and emotional. He uses unorthodox forms. He is imprecise and densely metaphorical. He is vague and impressionistic, preferring the drift of feelings to the march of reason. You might also want to add that at times he is shrill, hysterical and neurotic. Of course, such an assessment depends on a conventional evaluation of the 'feminine', but it is a useful starting-point. Luce Irigaray later claimed (as you will see in Section 3) that *écriture féminine* is non-argumentative. Lawrence, on the contrary, is obviously *very* argumentative. But just what are, or are not, the exact characteristics of masculinity and femininity (or indeed whether they *can* be exactly determined) is not my point. I want to suggest that if we look for gender in writing, we may find that it does not coincide with the biological sex of the writer.

2.4 But is writing gendered? Surely it would be surprising if it were not. What Virginia Woolf is getting at is that in writing, as in so much else, the masculine has been conflated with the norm. To me, Lawrence's writing (*The Virgin and the Gypsy* is almost contemporaneous with *A Room of One's Own*) communicates a sense of exuberance and relief in its freedom from the constraints of what was a 'normal' style.

2.5 Does this suggest that Lawrence was a 'feminine' writer – whether he wanted to be or not? He appears never to have been very secure in his own sexuality. Until quite recently, critics have ignored chronology in studying Lawrence's sexual theories, and failed to see that he was more than merely inconsistent – in fact he changed his views in relation to the changing times he lived in. Early in his life Lawrence sympathized with the suffragists and believed that rigorous distinctions between the sexes and their roles were psychologically damaging. At that time he actually endorsed a blurring of sexual identities, believing that men and women were each better for being a little of the other. Towards the end of his life, and after the war when illness had debilitated him, he became strident in advocating the primacy of maleness. Perhaps the content of his work becomes engaged in a subconscious contest with its form. His rhetorical strategies laid down minefields of impossible binds. To be unsubmissive was to be unfeminine and for men to lose their dominance was to endanger the future of civilization. Simone de Beauvoir observed that Lawrence's work consisted of 'guidebooks for women'. Kate Millett later pointed out that 'the heroines of [his] novels spend each book learning their part as females' (1977, p.286). What made him so insidious an enemy to women was that he paid them so much attention, claimed to feel like them, appeared to write from their point of view, *and even in their language*. Millett called him the most subtle of sexual politicians, 'for it is through a feminine consciousness that his masculine message is conveyed' (ibid., p.239).

Lawrence's misogyny

2.6 One of the ways in which Lawrence steered readers in his 'guidebooks for women' was by making it abundantly clear which course was to be avoided. The power of his writing makes his reader want very much *not* to be the kind of creature on whom he pours his contempt.

2.7 Aunt Cissie is presented as a diseased counterpart to Yvette, a woman in whom virginity has, in some unpleasant and maybe not entirely metaphorical sense (she has had 'an operation'), turned cancerous. Green is her colour – not of spring, but of gangrene. Her frustration has become a putrid sore: 'the helpless tumour of her rage was still running.' She is also (of course) menopausal:

> And now, she was creeping towards fifty, strange green flares of rage would come up in her, and at such times, she was insane.
>
> (p.9)

Realistically, there are very good reasons why the poor woman might be unhappy. She is the stay-at-home daughter, whose life has been 'sacrificed to the Mater'. She is even obliged to share her mother's bed:

> She prayed a good deal about it. Which also showed that she had her own private feelings somewhere, poor thing. She had ceased to be Cissie, she had lost her life and her sex.
>
> (p.9)

What those private feelings might be, Lawrence hardly troubles to explore. His attention to his characters' subconscious minds – which we shall look at in more detail later – is very selective. This passage marks the limit of his compassion. The rest is the narrator's disgust, which is quite disproportionate to the speech and actions directly attributed to the character. When, for example, she discovers that Yvette has borrowed the Window Fund, Lawrence turns her, with her 'grey-green mask', into some kind of vampire preying on the helpless recumbent virgin:

> ...the door softly opened, and there stood Aunt Cissie, pushing her grey-green face through the opening of the door. Yvette started up in terror...
>
> (p.33)

2.8 If you read the whole passage I think you will see that it is all too like something out of a horror movie. Until, that is, the last sentences: 'And amid it all, up came a bubble of distracted laughter. It *was* so filthily ridiculous!' The powerful instinct towards naturalism, which makes the depiction of Yvette in many ways so convincing, here supplies a corrective to excessive melodrama. But notice how recourse to the slang usage of 'filthily' allows Lawrence to have his cake and eat it: for Yvette it is just a modish exaggeration; for the narrative it reiterates the obscenity associated with Aunt Cissie.

2.9 The Window Fund offers, though it does not make explicit, a second possible source of her distress. The war, and the deaths the window is to commemorate, made marriage impossible for many of the generation of women whose potential partners were killed. Aunt Cissie is thus doubly victimized, yet she has lived through a period in which women's horizons were broadening. In the radio programme associated with this story, Hilary Simpson explains how the war years and the twenties had offered women employment opportunities, some political emancipation and the beginnings of freedom to control their reproductive capacities. Both Yvette and Lucille have been partly educated abroad; Lucille has a job; both have the comparative luxury of feeling that marriage is something they can postpone. Lawrence, however, claims that their freedom is specious: 'They seemed so free, and were as a matter of fact so tangled and tied up, inside themselves' (p.11). Yet Aunt Cissie, deprived of even the semblance of choice, is somehow the villain of the piece.

2.10 Inevitably, the war was followed by a reaction. Unemployment was a growing problem and men not unnaturally wanted to reclaim the jobs that women had taken over. But it went deeper than that. The war had not ended in a conclusive victory. It was a defeat for male, militaristic values, which reasserted themselves in a collective anxiety about what was seen as the threat of female dominance. Lawrence is not the only writer of the time to feel threatened by women. And while virginity is idealized by some religions (though Lawrence, as this story exemplifies, has little respect for the Church), it can also be seen as a challenge or reproach to an inadequate masculinity. Aunt Cissie's virgin/spinster state is partly the consequence of a failed masculine ethic, yet it is thrown back at her by the male narrator, and she is exhibited as a source of poison.

2.11 The other domineering monster in this story is 'the Mater', the sole victim of the cataclysm with which it ends. Here, some biographical information may be useful. *The Virgin and the Gypsy* was written shortly after Frieda Lawrence's grown-up daughters, from her first marriage, had visited their mother and seriously ill stepfather in Italy in 1925–6. In Frieda, the cult of the mother was writ large. In Germany, before she met Lawrence, she had been for a time the lover of Otto Gross, the leader of a group that called itself the 'Cosmic Circle' and claimed to stand for 'life-values, for eroticism, for the value of myth and primitive cultures, for the superiority of instinct and intuition to the values of science, for the primacy of the female mode of being' (Green, 1974). When he espoused Frieda, Lawrence for a time espoused these values too. Until he met her, the most powerful relationship in his life had been with his mother – a love he struggled with, but did not repudiate, and explored most famously in his early novel *Sons and Lovers* (1913) and the less autobiographical, more distanced work, *The Rainbow* (1915). In the foreword to *Sons and Lovers* he found a semi-mystical expression for the lure of the matriarchal:

> Yea, like bees in and out of a hive, we come backwards and forwards to our woman ... we are bees that go between, from the flower home to the hive and the Queen; for she lies at the centre of the hive, and stands in a way of bees for God the Father, the Almighty, the Unknowable, the Creator. In her all things are born, both words and bees.

2.12 But in *The Virgin and the Gypsy* this is replaced by the repulsive image of the Mater as a bee-eating toad, which:

> caught every bee as it came out to launch into the air, swallowed them one after the other, as if it could consume the whole hive-full, into its aged, bulging, purse-like wrinkledness.
>
> (p.18)

The mater-toad swallowing the emergent, new-born bees thus rewrote Lawrence's earlier beliefs. But he is famous, indeed celebrated, for his inconsistency. One of his greatest contributions to the changing art of the novel was his replacement of the old, stable notions of character with a much more fluid presentation of shifting internal landscapes. In his opinions, too, he was a mass of contradictions. But it is important to see that these changes were prompted not merely by his own changing circumstances and experience, but by pressures and intellectual developments to which his whole generation was subject.

The virgin

2.13 Lawrence's first-hand knowledge of Freud was limited, partly for the very good reason that some of Freud's major work was not available – or not even written – before Lawrence's death. But his impact was already widespread, and Lawrence knew at least as much about Freudianism as any other well-informed man of his generation. Indeed, he wrote two explicitly anti-Freudian works: *Psychoanalysis and the Unconscious* and *Fantasia of the Unconscious*, in which he argued against Freud's rationalism and maintained that a pre-rational *consciousness* needed to be re-awakened to govern our too 'mental' lives. Nevertheless, Freudian thinking, Freudian categories and assumptions are at work among the themes of this story.

2.14 Freud's name has been invoked many times in this course (for example in Block 4), but not even here is there room to do him justice. This is not a course on psychology or even twentieth-century thought. Inevitably Freud gets a raw deal here, because he is always introduced in relation to some other topic, and nowhere for himself. In relation to feminism, a more extensive treatment would be specially desirable – yet is specially difficult, so complex and divided are the responses to his work. Basically, it is very unclear whether Freud has been a friend to feminism or its enemy. I am sure it will be clear to you from what follows that I *tend* towards the latter view.

2.15 Freud saw passivity, masochism and narcissism as the three distinguishing characteristics of femininity. All three features are reflected in this story. He ascribed these traits not to social pressures and expectations but to a biological imperative: the lack of a penis. Not for a moment did it occur to him that what women might want was not the organ itself, but the privileges that apparently go with the possession of it. All his theories are predicated on the premise that the female knows herself to be incomplete. Where Freud introduced an enormous and beneficial change in our thinking was in his exploration of the nature of the subconscious, and the forces that operate there – a topic discussed in Block 4. It was he who systematically revealed how our actions are motivated by subconscious desires. But as far as women are concerned, he largely validated the status quo. Kate Millett described how, after Freud, Lawrence was able to construct theories about sexuality to endorse his masculine self-interest:

> Now it [could] be said scientifically that women are inherently subservient, and males dominant, more strongly sexed and therefore entitled to sexually subjugate the female, who enjoys her oppression and deserves it, for she is by her very nature, vain, stupid, and hardly better than barbarian, if she is human at all. Once this bigotry has acquired the cachet of science, the counter-revolution may proceed pretty smoothly.
>
> (Millett, op. cit., p.203)

Lawrence appears to bypass scientific theory and strike directly into Yvette's unconscious, but it is important to remember how new Freud's thinking was at the time, and how every reference to the unconscious would have invoked his theories. Lawrence's account of the various layers of Yvette's awareness may seem like mysticism (or flim-flam) to us; but to enthusiastic Freudians it may well have read like scientific analysis. Thus 'science' is invoked rather as 'Nature' was in the instance of the toad: both seem to lend credibility to the narrative. But have you ever heard of a toad eating bees? May not the science be as questionable as the natural history?

2.16 Freud's thinking about female sexuality in its virgin state also finds a powerful, though fragmented, reflection in Lawrence's story. Freud believed that, after the discovery of her own 'castration', the female inhibits all sexual activity, so that '...the major part of normal female youth was ... spent in a sexual limbo. The result is what a prurient patriarchy has always found so desirable, the virginal maiden utterly unsexual to herself' (Millet, op. cit., p.199). Yvette is passive to the extent that she barely responds to the pull of her subconscious needs. She visits the gypsy once on her own, but for all the narrative tells us, she might not know where she is going (p.51). There she is saved from the *moment critique* by the Eastwoods, who distract her from him for a time:

> She did not forget the gypsy entirely. But she had no time for him. She, who was bored almost to agony, and who had nothing at all to do, she had not time to think even, seriously.
>
> (p.74)

Yet it is Lawrence, ultimately, who doesn't quite wish to have Yvette seek out the gypsy lover he claims she needs. 'So, a *woman* could eat her cake and have her bread and butter', he says (p.75); but doesn't he do the same, as author? The flood washes away any deliberation in their coming together. And the gap in the text between parts nine and ten overwhelms what happens in Yvette's bed with authorial silence. This refusal to know on the author's part curiously mirrors the way in which Yvette is unknown to herself.

2.17 Yet Freud also maintained that the female virgin's sole need was for the sexual relationship that would supply her with the part she lacked and the babies that were a substitute for it. Thus she is a strangely vacant creature, craving what she is bound to inhibit and does not know. In this, as in much else, Freud ignored the social construction of sexuality, and failed to recognize that this limbo state was largely determined by social rather than natural prohibitions.

2.18 The masochism that Freud claimed was another female characteristic is here located in Yvette's relationship with her father, whose conduct towards her regarding the Eastwoods is distinctly sadistic. I expect you will have noticed how the daughter becomes elided in the fantasy of the mother, and the rector's threats against his daughter (including murder) are more proportionate to Cynthia's offence than to Yvette's mere indecorum. This fear of female sexuality is mired in the Victorian belief that 'depravity' leads to madness: '...certain tendencies end in criminal lunacy, unless they are curbed in time.' Freud's researches, on the other hand, had revealed that it was repression that lead to madness – and Aunt Cissie seems almost like a Freudian case-history, a classic case of masochism. The story holds together a spectrum of attitudes.

2.19 But the rector is not merely a sexual bully. In the same episode he is described as 'abject ... [backing] into the curtains, as if the girl menaced him with something fearful'. And he has fantasized the wound to his masculinity, inflicted by Cynthia, into the frozen prettiness of the snow-flower, turning pain into quasi-pleasure in a manner perhaps not unlike Aunt Cissie's martyrdom, and in itself masochistic. Though Lawrence at this stage of his life had come to believe that the differences between men and women needed to be reinforced, the story still enacts his earlier beliefs that there was no clear distinction between the sexes, and that both in varying degrees shared the other's characteristics. Yet it is perhaps just this old, stifling, unhealthy confusion (as he now sees it) that he wants to destroy in the flood.

2.20 *The Virgin and the Gypsy* was not, of course, intended as a Freudian exemplar. But the construction of Yvette presents the reader with a young woman in that combination of need and unknowing which represented not so much an eternal, natural verity as contemporary doctrine – an ideology as much subject to time and historical circumstances as (for example) Lawrence's anti-semitism, which regrettably we have no room to discuss.

2.21 And we must also remember that Lawrence was subject to the pressures of his time, which included still powerful prohibitions about what is now popularly known as 'explicit' sex. In some ways *The Virgin and the Gypsy* is a precursor to *Lady Chatterley's Lover* (1930), which is also about a high-born lady who finds the sexual fulfilment she needs with a man from a lower social class. That novel famously broke taboos with its use of forbidden words and relatively transparent descriptions of sexual acts. The earlier story can be seen as a 'virginal' treatment of the later novel, not just in the crude sense that it does not 'go so far', but in the reticence of its narrative.

2.22 In Block 4 it was suggested that silences can be as significant as inclusions. Now we want you to consider whether silences are gendered.

ACTIVITY

The Virgin and the Gypsy is not a simple, doctrinaire narrative. It consists of many strands that are woven together, yet sometimes in a contradictory tension, and we can understand Lawrence's methods better if we look at how the strands are combined in a complete section. Please re-read part five ('It was nearly tea-time...', pp.40–50).

How is landscape used to enhance the erotic tension?

DISCUSSION

With restraint. It certainly doesn't thrust and throb with sexual meaning in the way that Stella Gibbons parodied in *Cold Comfort Farm*. But a good novelist does not merely add background for its own sake. The 'things' in a story are as eloquent as the characters. And the rectory in its wooded, watery valley, with the road that Yvette 'always expected *something* to come down', is quietly suggestive at the same time as it is a realistic description of a Northern dale. Beyond this sheltered, tender spot are 'the grim stone mills ... their tall chimneys long and erect'.

If you look at the descriptive attributes ascribed to both Yvette and the gypsy you can see that this contrast is extended into the depiction of both. She is still, half-naked and chilly at the window. He is moving, 'limber', 'alert' – and festooned with discreetly naturalistic phallic symbols: 'long duster-brooms of reed and feather ... nodding on their stalks of cane' and a candlestick with a 'low, thick stem of copper, rising from a double bowl'. Not surprisingly, he has Aunt Cissie 'fluttered'. All the apparently insignificant details of place, actions and things are helping to enact the sexual drama. But of course, as you know, there is no such thing as insignificant detail. When the gypsy opens 'the white gate', Lawrence is making the detail mirror the whole.

ACTIVITY

Part five is divided into three carefully contrasted episodes: the gypsy's visit, the girls dressing-up for dinner and the party. These represent Yvette's options: the gypsy, home and marriage. I have already referred to the second episode, but look at it again (pp.44–6).

What does Lawrence use it to achieve?

DISCUSSION

The crucial paragraph begins: 'She was truly simple in what she said...' (p.45), and it contrasts Yvette's 'outside' and her 'inside'. The party clothes and the rather desperate party behaviour represent her surface limits, the extreme point of contrast with the seething, inarticulate silence and need within. In Freudian terms this is, of course, the contrast between the conscious and the unconscious modes of being.

And it is not only a contrast, but a conflict. Yvette wants to 'counteract the effect the gypsy had had on her'. She retreats to the surface, admiring her own beauty in a brief narcissistic orgy which, in terms of Freud's argument, evinces yet again the female's hopeless desire to be male, since she is regarding *herself* in the way that properly belongs to the male. Thus in Freudian terms, the very action consciously intended to *counteract* the gypsy enacts her desire for him, and the more she tries to escape from her sexual destiny (and for Freud there isn't any other for a woman), the more she is drawn towards it.

But at the same time, of course, the episode dramatizes a need for an escape that is perhaps more feasible: from the drab gentility of the rectory. The dressing-up is both a suppression and an *expression* and it is this ambivalence that must exonerate Lawrence partially from Millett's charges against him. This story, after all, does not end with any kind of claim to have provided a solution for Yvette's dilemma. It would have been mere fantasy to suggest that she could have made a life with the gypsy. Even in *Lady Chatterley's Lover* sexual fulfilment is not the be-all and end-all, but a source of new energy for social endeavour that had previously been stifled. Lawrence shows himself to be fully aware that Yvette is as frustrated by her society as by her virginity. He consistently endorses the aspirations of his female characters towards a fuller life. Where feminists must part company with him is that he seeks to impose male-determined limits on those aspirations, and that he habitually shows women as incapable of realizing their fulfilment without male intervention. Thus Yvette can do nothing active for herself: the gypsy resuscitates and releases her; and Lawrence supplies the act of God which destroys the rectory and its usurping female deity.

ACTIVITY

The third episode (pp.47–50) is a fine piece of social comedy. Leo (a bit of a lion) is 'a sort of mastiff among the house-dogs ... with fresh cheery-o! courage', is typical of his class, not a bad chap as far as he goes, but utterly lacking the gypsy's blatant sexuality. Look carefully through this last part for examples of how Yvette's sexuality is defined.

DISCUSSION

They are very numerous. She has 'no idea' of her effect on Leo; she is 'lost in amazement', as if the thought of romance (at a *party*? what else is that kind of party for?) hadn't occurred to her. All her instant, reactive thoughts of the gypsy are promptly repudiated, as the conscious censors the unconscious mind. She is lonely and fastidious, spiteful and – in Leo's eyes – finally both catty and bitchy. She is also oddly absent-minded, as if in some kind of trance – or not yet fully awakened – and of course, earlier in the episode and elsewhere, she is referred to as being in a kind of sleep, like the Lady of Shalott.

All this amounts to what is, when you look at it, a very strange construction of female sexuality. And 'construction' (not depiction) is the right word, for it is built up out of a collection of disparate elements, which Lawrence cements together with his repeated use of the word 'virgin'. We have, quite literally, to take his word for it that this is what virginity is like. But is it? Is this a naturalistic portrait? Desire and passivity are surely a paradoxical combination, expressing not so much a psychic imperative as a male fantasy of the passive female who does not know what she needs. And this would be naturalistic – if you believe Freud to be right.

But if Freud was in error in attributing repression entirely to nature and not to social conditioning, there is a strange hiatus here. For the material of the story half-suggests that the sources of repression can indeed be located in society, yet does not quite make the connection. Yvette's 'sleep' is not ascribed to residual Victorian prudery forbidding her to acknowledge her sexual needs, but is seen as endemic to virginity and thus somehow transcendent. Lawrence was both a mystic and an astute social observer. Indeed, it was the latter trait that lead him to conclude that the lives of his contemporaries fatally lacked a spiritual dimension. Having rejected familiar religions, he was not alone in trying to locate the mystical and the transcendent in sex. In this respect he ran counter to Freud, whose endeavour was to demystify and systematize.

The gypsy

2.23 I have suggested that whether Yvette is 'realistic' or not depends on your ideology. But there is no such ambivalence about the gypsy: he is a fantasy figure. Hilary Simpson somewhat iconoclastically compares Lawrence's use of such figures with Edith Maud Hull's *The Sheik*, memorably filmed in 1921 with Rudolf Valentino in the leading role. We usually think of such figures as aimed at female readers or as the projections of female novelists. But I don't think there can be much doubt that the gypsy was a potent fantasy for Lawrence too, and that he expected his male readers to be stirred by it. And in this respect, the narrative itself can be seen to be narcissistic – the male author is admiring his own sex and masculine beauty in the way that 'properly' belongs to the female. I am not, of course, saying there's anything wrong with this. Far from it. Since I incline more towards Lawrence's earlier belief that gender is a continuum rather than a hard and fast difference, I enjoy the ways in which the narrative tends towards the 'feminine' despite its overt intentions.

2.24 You may also have thought there was something rather 'feminine' about the attention Lawrence gives to the gypsy's appearance – as much as to the sisters' silks and satins. His pleasure in clothes is one of his most engaging characteristics. In most other respects, however, the gypsy is almost a parody of maleness. We are, for example, given absolutely nothing about his unconscious. The effect, carefully constructed, is not to make us think that he's too shallow to have one, but partly that he's too mysterious to be penetrated, and partly that his quintessential masculinity has made him all of a piece, so that there is no disjunction between what he seems and what he is. The unconscious being a messy, secret sort of place, it's no wonder that the fantasy male should be without one, whereas in Yvette it is the location of her quintessential femininity.

2.25 We are also told nothing about the physical effect she has on him, though a line like 'the surface of her body seemed to turn to water' (p.27) is typical of *her* response. (And it's also typical of the cheapest fiction.) I am sure you can work out the ideological implications of this distinction.

2.26 It is also typical of a fantasy that he should be a social outcast. By not being part of the conventional group, he not only offers a critique of it, but confirms his status as a fantasy, something outside and beyond the everyday, on whom no claims can be made. Disdain – the gypsy is constantly sneering or contemptuous in expression – is a commonplace feature of such characters, not merely because women, as masochists, are supposed to like being despised but because it prevents the character from putting down roots in the society he quite arbitrarily enters and leaves. Yet if Lawrence believed that the English bourgeoisie needed the direct transfusion of masculine sexuality that the gypsy represents, it is not quite satisfactory to have him come and go. He was to find a better resolution in *Lady Chatterley's Lover*.

2.27 The ending of the story is a *tour de force* and here the gypsy seems to emerge from the rather cardboardy peacock into a more rounded and believable character, though the sexual stereotyping persists and Yvette is more or less passively helpless until he 'commands'. It is she, however, who asks him into her bed: '"Warm me!" she moaned, with chattering teeth. "Warm me! I shall die of shivering." There is, of course, another, more metaphysical cold that endangers her life, and from which, we are to assume, he also saves her. Yet interestingly, what follows is evasive. And it is surely not voluntary censorship that deters Lawrence, and makes him end the episode in sleep rather than sex. He is a master of unspecific erotica which leaves the reader in no doubt about what is taking place under a blanket of sometimes overblown prose. But here, in resisting the predictable, he achieves something more richly ambiguous. Perhaps he feels an authorial delicacy about the virginity he has been at such pains to construct. Perhaps he wants to suggest that it is in shared warmth and unconscious sympathy, rather than merely the sexual act, that the crucial transference of the gypsy's vitality is better effected. Maybe he thought that sex would not have given him an ending. He chose to conclude on an oddly mundane note – the gypsy's name – which cancels out a lesser textual silence, while leaving the larger silence intact.

3 *Psychoanalysis and language*

The growth of psychoanalysis: Freud

3.1 Even if you have never read a word of psychoanalytic theory, it has affected your understanding of the world. Women – and men – now see themselves differently because of what psychoanalysis has had to say about the force of the unconscious mind, the significance of dreams, the nature of infant sexuality or repression. But feminists have disagreed sharply in their interpretations of its significance. Has it been useful to women – a means by which the slow processes of understanding and liberation have been advanced? Or has psychoanalysis turned out to be yet another way of perpetuating women's subordination? Could it be both? As the preceding section has suggested, the debate has a long and sometimes complicated history. And in Radio 14 *Feminist Debates*: *psychoanalysis*, Toril Moi and Janet Todd outline the central issues. In its most recent developments the argument has focused on the nature of language. Does psychoanalysis reveal that women are alienated from the linguistic structures of our culture at the very deepest levels? This is a proposition that has had far-reaching consequences for feminist thinking about literature.

3.2 One of the areas in which Simone de Beauvoir's *The Second Sex* was most iconoclastic was in its distrustful view of the theories of Sigmund Freud (1856–1939), the father of modern psychoanalysis. De Beauvoir pointed out that Freud's apparently objective theories were in fact profoundly influenced by unrecognized suppositions about the nature and proper role of women. She argues that these assumptions were pervasively misogynist. Freudian feminists have since contended that de Beauvoir's animosity was based on a misreading, and that Freud was far from proposing an essential inferiority in women. In their eyes, Freud's contribution to women's advantage has lain in the central part he played in the intellectual revolution that has allowed their work to flourish. Freud's sense of gender as a constructed concept, always problematic and unstable, was an indispensable starting-point for the development of feminist theory.

3.3 But de Beauvoir was not a trained psychoanalyst. To the eye of the sceptical outsider, ideas such as penis envy, female narcissism and female masochism seemed less than promising as a means of furthering the cause of women's dignity and independence. In this, as in so many other respects, de Beauvoir's thinking was amplified in Millett's *Sexual Politics*. Millett's attack on Freud was one of the most enjoyably vituperative aspects of her book. Throughout the seventies, most North American feminist critics accepted the arguments of Millett and her followers, and were either hostile or indifferent to the influence of Freud's work.

3.4 The French successors of de Beauvoir took a different attitude. Of the many differences that evolved between feminism in the USA during this period, and feminism as it developed in France, the attitude towards psychoanalysis was the most momentous. Although they shared de Beauvoir's inclination towards philosophy, and her tendency to universalize her examination of the situation of women rather than place it in a specific historical context, French feminists after de Beauvoir did not share her view of Freud. Feminists could not, they argued, afford to reject Freud's major innovation: the idea of the unconscious and its influence on conscious behaviour. Hélène Cixous put the case for Freud in a conversation recorded in 1986:

> Fifteen years ago, Freud was prohibited in feminist circles, on the pretext that he was a misogynist. At the time I wondered how these feminists could possibly hope to get through life because everything had been invented by men. It was like saying, 'we can't go by plane because a woman didn't invent it'. Freud focussed attention on the unconscious in an extraordinary series of discoveries. Do we behave as if the unconscious didn't exist? We live in a post-Freudian, Derridean age of electricity and the aeroplane. So let's do as modern people do, let's use the contemporary means of transport. We owe Freud the exploration of the unconscious.
>
> (quoted in Sellers, 1988, pp. 144–5)

Why should Freud's theories about the activities of the unconscious mind be of any special value to feminists? This is a question that you are already in a position to begin to answer. The concept of the unconscious implies a powerful critique of the idea that rational mental processes necessarily govern our thoughts and actions. However successful we are in convincing ourselves that we are in control of what we do, or what we believe, we are in fact driven by motives and experiences hidden in inaccessible regions of the mind – so the Freudian argument runs. If you look back over what we have said so far about the central preoccupations of the feminist movement, you will see how feminists have wished to question the dominance of reason and logic. The thinking of Freud has been a powerful ally in this challenge. The perception of the unconscious has allowed women to write about contradiction and confusion, ambivalence and silence. Of course, it has also enabled men to do the same thing, in ways that have not always been sympathetic to feminist thinking. The expressive qualities of silence are not confined to women, nor are women alone in wishing to write about the deep compulsions that lie unrecognized behind our apparently rational actions. This is a point that was raised in Block 3 Section 3, and it is clearly important to your understanding of D.H. Lawrence's *The Virgin and the Gipsy*. It is one we will return to when we come to consider Hemingway's story 'The Short Happy Life of Francis Macomber'.

3.5 It would be wrong to give the impression that Freud has been the only means through which the smooth surfaces of logic have been fractured, as your encounters with the thinking of Althusser and Macherey in Block 4 will have shown you. There have been other routes leading to the recognition of the gaps and omissions in any discourse. Here Freud's giant shadow mixes with that of Marx, who had also argued that the true significance of social activity was hidden from the consciousness or the control of the individual. Marxist critics, like feminists, have had reason to cultivate an awareness of what is not said. And the political insights of Marxism have made it easier for us to discern other voices which have been silenced alongside those of women: those of the poor, or of black people. The issues of race and gender converge through the mediation of Marxism and feminism.

Poststructuralist psychoanalysis: Lacan

3.6 The feminist potential in psychoanalysis seemed still more fruitful in the light of the work of the French Freudian revisionist, Jacques Lacan (1901–86). The notoriously baffling territory of Lacan's psychoanalytic theory initially appears quite as inhospitable to feminists as that of Freud. Indeed, it might seem still less encouraging, for Lacan goes much further than Freud in claiming a dominant status for the phallus in the development of the human psyche. Lacan was by no means a feminist – his scorn of the movement is well known. Nevertheless, his thought has had a fundamental influence on feminist approaches to literature. One reason for this is that he renders Freud's analysis of the workings of the unconscious into relentlessly linguistic terms, thus reinforcing the perception of gender as a socially constructed concept rather than a biological destiny. For Lacan, women and men can exist only in language, the place where their identity is perpetually in the process of being constructed. It is in the work of Lacan that psychoanalysis confronts the complexities of language and gender most directly.

3.7 Clarity of expression, never among Lacan's primary characteristics, often disappears altogether when his work is translated. This is partly due to his penchant for puns, a rhetorical device that can rarely be translated. The same difficulty characterizes the writing of his followers, some of whom raise Lacan's work to heights of opacity undreamed of by Lacan himself. But the punning obscurities of Lacan and Lacanians are not simply a perverse barrier erected to deter the uninitiated from the mysteries of thought they conceal. They cannot be separated from what Lacan is trying to do, which is why simplifying summaries of his thought – like the one that you are about to read – must always be to some extent a betrayal of his intellectual project. No one finds his work easy, but many find it illuminating – particularly with regard to questions of women's language. It's worth making an effort to try to see why he has had such an impact on feminist thought. You will find further help with the issues raised by Lacan's ideas in Radio 14. I want now to try to do two things – firstly, to give you some idea of what Lacan is saying; secondly, to ponder the question of why so many active feminists have been ready to listen.

3.8 What was Lacan getting at? The starting-point of his work lies in his famous assertion that the unconscious is structured like a language. This link has crucial implications for both language and the unconscious. Language can express no fixed relationship to a concept existing in reality. Its meaning is relative, placed within a network of shifting associations and connections. If we are not aware of these connections, it is often because we repress them. But they emerge in the texture of our writing and speech – as, for instance, in the apparently arbitrary associations made in puns. In asserting the instability of language, Lacanian psychoanalysis is closely associated with the French school of philosophical thought headed by the poststructuralist theorist Jacques Derrida (b.1930). It can sometimes be hard to disentangle the influence of Lacan from that of Derrida, whose authority carries comparable weight – so we need to pause briefly here to consider how Lacan's position relates to that of Derrida.

3.9 Derrida builds on the seminal work of the Swiss linguist Ferdinand de Saussure (1857–1913) and, like Lacan, denies that language can provide direct access to reality. Saussure contends that language is a system of meaning built on difference: words and meaning have no more than an arbitrary connection. Language, in Saussurean terms, is a *structure*, whose parts can only be understood in relation to each other. Saussure's theories became the foundation of structuralist thought. But Derrida, a poststructuralist, goes still further. He asserts that the connection is not only arbitrary, it is also volatile. For Derrida, all meaning is temporary and relative, definable only in the context of a specific linguistic event, located in a relation of difference with all other linguistic events. The concept of *différance* – the idea that meaning is both product of differences between signifiers and always subject to deferral[1]– is fundamental to the philosophy of Derrida. It amounts to a repudiation of the tradition of rationalist thought – a tradition that depended on the belief that meaning could exist independently of its articulation in language.

3.10 Lacan, as a psychoanalyst rather than a philosopher, places the emphasis elsewhere. For him, unconscious desire, rather than *différance*, is what precludes absolute fixity in meaning. His theory is based on an account of the ways in which the growing child has to recognize and cope with the knowledge of its separate identity, distinct first from the mother's body, and then from the complex physical and social world in which it finds itself. According to Lacan, this process inevitably takes place in the context of unfulfilled desire, as the recognition of separation, beginning with the experience of the intermittent withdrawal of the mother's breast, must imply desire for what cannot be possessed. This desire comes to express itself through the mastery of language. Through language, the child is eventually able to deal with unsatisfied desire by creating an illusion of control. Lacan argues that this is because language enables the child to identify itself with the 'Other', which becomes the location of power, authority and meaning. The concept of the 'Other' is therefore as important to Lacan as to de Beauvoir. But it assumes a rather different (though not unrelated) function in his thinking. De Beauvoir saw the 'Other' as the site of what is mysterious, unreachable, alien. For Lacan, it comes to represent that which is desired, the position of strength with which the child identifies, thus laying claim to control over what is beyond itself. In these terms, the 'Other' becomes the place where language is to be found. Words are thus more than a medium of communication for Lacan: they are the means by which the child comes to terms with the isolation and powerlessness of human existence.

3.11 How does language come to perform this vital function? What Lacan terms the 'mirror stage' is the first step towards gaining an illusory sense of control. The young child, not yet able to speak, identifies with the image of itself reflected in the mirror. Lacan is using the mirror metaphorically here, to signify the image of itself that the child perceives around it. Identifying with the image involves a split in identity between the 'I' who watches and the 'I' who is watched. But the child, observing with satisfaction that it can control the reflected image, sees no such split. A unity between the self and the image is imagined. So this stage becomes, as Lacan describes it, the 'imaginary' stage. Later, the child must leave the comfort of the imaginary stage in order to approach what Lacan calls the 'symbolic order', i.e. the world of social community and conformity: language, law, order and institution. Only then can the process of becoming a speaking adult enter its final phase. It is at the point of entry into the symbolic order that the function of gender in its relation to language becomes crucial in Lacan's theory.

3.12 The full realization of separation from the mother comes through the intervention of the father – or the externally ordered world which the father represents – symbolized, in Lacan's terms, by the phallus. In this version of Freud's Oedipus complex, the phallus becomes the 'transcendental signifier', that is, it represents the symbolic order, preventing the child from lingering within the imaginary phase. Like the mirror, the phallus has an abstract function here: it is not identical with the penis. Representing a symbolic order which includes language, it has itself become a symbol – a gendered marker of division and exclusion. The child copes with the sense of loss implied by the usurping father as it had coped with the division between itself and its image in the mirror stage – by claiming a specious unity between itself and

[1]The French word carries both meanings – difference and deferral.

what it imagines it can control. Occupying the position of the 'Other', here identified with the symbolic order or the phallus, allows the child to see itself as a source of language, as having the ability to govern meaning. This supposed capacity seems to promise that the wholeness experienced in the imaginary phase can be recaptured. This is an illusion, just as the unity that the child saw between itself and its image in the 'mirror stage' was an illusion: in fact the child can never fuse with the 'Other', and its motivating desire is doomed never to be satisfied. Language, then, for Lacan, is inseparably bound up with pain and loss. Derrida had pointed to the absence at the centre of language; Lacan translated this absence into a sombre experience that every child must undergo. In becoming socialized adults, we are propelled into an endless process of deferred desire, moving from one signifier to another. Language, a product of desire, is also an inescapably gendered phenomenon, an expression of lack which is never to be fulfilled.

3.13 What has all this got to offer feminists? Precious little, you might well be feeling, if you have managed to pick your way through the paragraphs above. Lacan, after all, is insisting that it is only through the concept of the phallus – here an abstract rather than a physical appendage, but nevertheless unquestionably male – and the devaluation and rejection of the mother, that the child is able to become a speaking adult. In Lacan's thought, all power is focused on the phallus. If it is the 'universal signifier', what role remains for women? Why should they trouble themselves any further with what Lacan had to say?

3.14 It seems that women used Lacan's theories as they used Freud's. Lacan offered a large and complex body of thought from which they could single out what they needed. The central reason for his pervasive and lasting presence as an intellectual force within feminism and his most significant contribution to feminist thought, lies in his analysis of gender identity as a cultural construct, as something that is always fragmented, always unstable. This is why Lacan has continued to matter to feminist thought. But he also formulated and dignified concepts that were significant to women for quite different reasons. Take, for instance, the idea of gazing into a mirror. As a metaphor for human experience, it suggests a passivity and self-absorption that has made it traditionally a feminine image (mermaids, the lady of Shalott...), rather than anything a man might decently be caught doing. Now Lacan was suggesting that, metaphorically, mirror-gazing was an indispensable stage in human development. Like Freud, Lacan offered an understanding of the human condition that was firmly based on the individual as a member of the family, rather than the wider community – and the family had always been a feminine province. It is worth noting here that the inward life of the individual, rather than the public life of the state, has always been attractive to poets and novelists too: in this respect, psychoanalysis and literature have shared the same territory.

3.15 The idea of a hidden world, distinct from the forces of political history but focused instead on the deep distresses of the inner life, was not new to women. Centuries of experience had already taught them something about desire, absence and loss. Feminist or not, they had good historical reasons to feel alienated from history and to be concerned with the experiences, and sometimes creative results, of exclusion and pain. Now Lacan seemed to be saying that it was not, after all, the public landscapes of history that mattered most. It was what had been confined to the female – lack, difference and desire, conditions not defined by rationality – that, in Lacan's analysis, was turning out to set the universal parameters of human experience, and of language itself. It made a change for women to be able to see these dark currents as central, rather than peripheral, elements of the intellectual world, and it was a change that many found liberating.

3.16 There were other reasons for the status of Lacan in avant-garde feminism during the seventies and eighties. Some of these had a great deal more to do with the nature of academic life – for Lacan has always been a quintessentially academic figure – than with the popular foundations of the movement. You have noted the importance of Lacan's attack on logic, and that this was the source of his attraction for feminists. But the attack was not couched in anything approaching anti-intellectual terms. Far from it. The sheer difficulty of Lacan (and Derrida: here again, the association is a close one) made the mastery of his thought seem a public proof of intelligence. The unspoken implication was often that those who indignantly rejected Lacan's authority (including most established male literary academics aged over forty), did so because they were not equipped with the powerful and subtle intelligence needed to comprehend him. Many a young female academic, struggling to make a career in a difficult environment, found such an assumption rather cheering. This was one of the ways in which Lacan was most valuable to feminists. He was a source of cultural confidence and authority, conferring the power to put masculine institutions on the defensive. Lacanian psychoanalysis acquired an image comparable with that of existentialism a generation earlier – it was glamorous, French, daring and rebellious. In this way the obscurity of Lacan, accentuated in the writing of his followers, was an important source of his prestige, rather than an impediment.

3.17 Nevertheless, the problem of the idea of language as the province of the symbolic order represented by the phallus, which seemed an inescapably patriarchal notion, remained. In order to deal with the problem, French feminists have proposed the concept of a language that is *not* controlled by patriarchal law. I want now to look at the idea of feminine writing, or *écriture féminine*, as a response to the masculine orientation of psychoanalytic theory.

Ecriture féminine: Kristeva, Irigaray and Cixous

3.18 Disconcertingly, the three French women who have had most to contribute to the debate about *écriture féminine* have not wished to call themselves feminists. Nor are they primarily literary critics. Julia Kristeva (b.1941) is a philosopher, Luce Irigaray (b.1939) a psychoanalyst, Hélène Cixous (b.1937) a creative writer and playwright. These women are sympathetic to the feminist movement, and lend their support to its aims with varying degrees of enthusiasm. But they have often voiced a suspicion of its political activities, because they consider the wish for social reform to be tainted with the patriarchal values of the symbolic order. They argue that such reform, though desirable, can never be more than superficial. Similarly, they have no interest in reconstructing past traditions of women's writing. Such a project strikes them as an acceptance of the terms of the same patriarchal order that was initially to blame for marginalizing women, since all women have been constrained to write within the phallocentric realm. Their project is a more radical one. They want to reconstruct our understanding of the world, our beliefs and actions and the language in which they are expressed, at the very deepest level. Only then, they insist, will the aspirations of feminists be satisfied, for they will have become redundant.

3.19 Do such utopian ambitions bear any realistic relationship to women's aspirations? Or, from the more specific point of view of our own work, will they help us form a clearer idea of the role of gender in the processes of writing and reading literature? To try to answer these questions, we have to start with some very basic premises.

Kristeva

3.20 Kristeva, Irigaray and Cixous have all followed Derrida in wishing to disrupt the oppositional patterns of thinking that they see as responsible for the rigidity of our interpretations of the human experience. The most significant of these binary oppositions sets male against female. But others are grouped around that basic antagonism: culture/nature, active/passive, light/dark, sun/moon, head/heart. These antitheses derive their structure from a hierarchy of power. The male element is seen as strong and positive, while the female is cast as negative and weak. This underlying pattern has become one of the most fundamental ways in which philosophy (and literature) has organized its understanding of the world. In challenging what they feel has become a strait-jacket of thought, Kristeva, Irigaray and Cixous want to challenge the foundations of our apprehensions of gender. Here's Kristeva:

> The belief that 'one is a woman' is almost as absurd and obscurantist as the belief that 'one is a man'. I say 'almost' because there are many goals which women can achieve: freedom of abortion and contraception, day-care centres for children, equality on the job, etc. Therefore we must use 'we are women' as an advertisement or slogan for our demands. On a deeper level, however, a woman cannot 'be'; it is something which does not even belong in the order of being. It follows that a feminist practice can only be negative, at odds with what already exists so that we may say 'that's not it' and 'that's still not it'. In 'woman' I see something that cannot be represented, something that is not said, something above and beyond nomenclatures and ideologies.
>
> (in Marks and de Courtivron, 1981, p.137)

Kristeva, a philosopher, seems here to be denying the tools of her own trade. Woman cannot be defined. Nor, apparently, can man. But this assertion springs from her distrust of definition itself, and from her modification of Lacan's ideas about the nature of language.

3.21 What did Kristeva say about language? Taking Lacan's analysis as a starting-point, Kristeva adds a dimension that changes the whole direction of his argument. She accepts that the language of the law – definition and control – is located within the symbolic realm, as Lacan had claimed. But she posits the existence of another kind of language, for which she adopts the term 'semiotic'. This language is not an alternative to the phallocentric language of the law: it is contained within it, as a pressure modifying the separation and fixity that she sees as characterizing the symbolic function. It is anarchic, disruptive, irresponsible and joyous, perpetually overturning the sombre structures of power that Lacan had described. One of the major advantages of Kristeva's concept of the semiotic is that it allows some possibility of escape from the unremitting gloom of Lacan's linguistic model. In this respect Kristeva and her followers appropriate an idea that has its origins in the work of the French writer Roland Barthes (1915–1980): the concept of *jouissance*, or the 'pleasure of the text'.

3.22 As far as Kristeva is concerned, the major reason for the generous fertility of the semiotic is that it is grounded in the presence of the mother. Before entering the realm of the symbolic, which is also the realm of the father, the child has no language. But it is aware of a rhythmic, wordless flow of drives, or appetites. These drives, which Kristeva calls 'pulsions', are gathered in a *chora* (from the Greek word for receptacle, or womb). They constitute a form of language, though the tide of experience they represent is without organized meaning or expression at this point. The child's only language is a cry. This semiotic flow must be repressed to permit the articulation of structured speech. But, like all repressed experience, it re-emerges in uncontrollable ways. The semiotic becomes a subversive force within the ordered social world of which language is a part. The *chora* is the embodiment, in words, of ambivalence, confusion, fecundity, absence, silence and disorder. Its presence is not always a soft, comfortingly maternal flow of words: it may be threatening, even sadistic. But it is intimately associated with the child's earliest experience of the mother's nurturing body. It is always fertile, always opposed to the hard outlines of the phallocentric order. It perpetually undermines that which organizes and controls our experience. According to Kristeva, the semiotic impulse takes an exuberant delight in its repudiation of structures like those of religion, social institutions, formal education, ownership, and so forth.

3.23 Kristeva did not claim that the semiotic is the property of women, any more than Lacan had asserted that the symbolic realm is the province of men. The opposition between male and female does not exist, she argues, before the entry into the symbolic order: therefore semiotic language must be without gender. Nevertheless, it is clear that its maternal origins imply a close association with the feminine, just as Lacan's phallic 'transcendental signifier' is inevitably linked with the masculine. Kristeva insists that her idea of a semiotic language is by no means identical with *écriture féminine*, though the two concepts share many significant features. It is not hard to see the attraction that her theory had for feminist literary critics. Here was a way of talking about what had already begun to preoccupy them: women's writing as a source of questioning, a challenge to the domination of the masculine systems of institution and law.

3.24 But how might Kristevan ideas of the semiotic conceivably be useful to our attempt to arrive at a richer understanding of the development of literature in the modern world? Is it of any interest to anyone other than a Parisian intellectual? To try to answer this question, I want to pause to reconsider passages from two texts already familiar to you.

ACTIVITY

The passages I want to look at occur in Virginia Woolf's *Mrs Dalloway* (pp.72–5, where Peter Walsh and Rezia Smith encounter the old woman outside Regent's Park Tube Station) and Forster's *A Passage to India* (pp.124–5: the description of the Marabar Caves; and pp.145–8: Mrs Moore's response to hearing the echo in the caves). Read them carefully, thinking particularly about the kind of language represented in the old woman's song and the echo of the caves. Then ask yourself the following:

(a) Do Forster and Woolf seem to you to be writing about something comparable in these passages?

(b) Does either author's writing have any connection, in these instances, with Kristeva's concept of semiotic language?

Make notes of your response.

DISCUSSION

(a) The passages are very different – but they do seem to have some significant points in common. What did you notice?

One obvious point is that both the old woman's song and the cave's echo are placed outside meaning, though they are language of a sort – 'boum', 'ee um fah um so...'. Clearly this is language quite oblivious to the rules of grammar, though not incapable of communication.

The second point that strikes me is that the old woman's song and the caves' echo are both placed in an unimaginably remote period of history – or, more accurately, prehistory. Both seem to predate human culture. The echo seems to predate life itself.

Not only do the echo and the song seem to predate human society, they make its concerns irrelevant. At least, they suggest something of the kind to those who hear them. This is particularly true of Mrs Moore's reaction to the echo: 'Pathos, piety, courage – they exist, but are identical, and so is filth. Everything exists, nothing has value' (p.147). But Rezia's response is comparable, though rather more cheerful. The old woman's song urges her to stop giving 'meanings to things that happened ... It was a silly, silly dream, being unhappy' (p.75).

I would also want to argue that both the echo and the song are associated with femaleness in a physical sense. Forster's description of the caves makes their likeness to female anatomy very clear – they consist of a tunnel leading to a circular chamber; they have skin 'finer than any covering acquired by the animals, smoother than windless water, more voluptuous than love' (p.125). Lighting a match in these caves seems to be something like making love: 'the radiance increases, the flames touch one another, kiss, expire' (p.125). The old woman, singing about her nameless lover, also seems to represent the female body:

> still, though it issued from so rude a mouth, a mere hole in the earth, muddy too, matted with root fibres and tangled grasses, still the old bubbling burbling song, soaking through the knotted roots of infinite ages, and skeletons and treasure, streamed away in rivulets over the pavement and all along the Marylebone Road, and down towards Euston, fertilizing, leaving a damp stain.

(b) In a sense, you will have answered the second of the questions I proposed in thinking about the first. It does seem clear that the anarchic language of both the caves and the old woman might be described in terms of Kristeva's idea of the semiotic. It is interesting, to press the comparison a little further, to see that the caves' echo is specifically placed in opposition to Christianity, defined by Kristeva as the ultimate home of the law of the father – and that this opposition is expressed in linguistic terms: 'But suddenly, at the edge of her mind, Religion appeared, poor little talkative Christianity, and she knew that all its divine words from "Let there be Light" to "It is finished" only amounted to "boum"' (p.148). The old woman, too, doesn't sound much like a church-goer.

But it is also clear, I think, that some problems remain. Do feminists really want to identify their language with burbles and booms? Obviously, neither Woolf nor Forster did. The caves' echo is a nihilistic threat: whatever else it may have in common with Kristeva's *chora*, it doesn't seem to offer much in the way of *jouissance*. Woolf's old woman might seem rather more consoling. But I don't think Woolf really manages to keep the disgust out of her voice when she speaks of that muddy hole in the ground. And semiotic language does raise some awkward political questions when it emerges from a begging woman. The right-thinking Rezia gets to the heart of the matter here, as so often in the novel: '...where did she sleep at night?'

3.25 I'm not really being fair here, since any expression of the semiotic in a novel must inevitably be shaped by the identity of the novelist. Forster and Woolf both had their own reasons for feeling nervous about women's bodies. Perhaps the point is not so much to hunt out isolated examples of the semiotic – after all, Kristeva emphasized its identity as a pressure *within* language, rather than an alternative *kind* of language – as to be alert to the places in a text where its disruptive forces make themselves manifest. Do any such moments come to your mind? We might look for them particularly in poetry, perhaps – a discourse, Kristeva claims, that must finally depend on the semiotic rather than the symbolic resources of language (this is a point that you will find interesting to consider in relation to your earlier work on Jakobson's view of poetic language in Block 2 Section 6). In Eliot's *The Waste Land*, perhaps? Does 'Shantih, shantih, shantih' (line 433) approach a semiotic energy? Or – a rather more unlikely candidate – in the poetry of Larkin, who writes in 'Here' about 'unfenced existence: Facing the sun, untalkative, out of reach' (Poetry Anthology)?

3.26 I have said that Kristeva's semiotic language is not identical with *écriture féminine*. How, then, does it differ? The central difference lies in Kristeva's insistence that it has the power to operate as a disruptive force within the symbolic order, whereas the proponents of *écriture féminine* usually see it as an order of language existing outside patriarchal discourse, on the margins of culture. Its speakers are to be seen as revolutionaries outside the gates, rather than as subversives within. You might imagine that it also differs in that it may be discerned in the writing of men, as well as women. After all, Forster, Eliot and Larkin hardly seem the likeliest authors of *écriture féminine* (Larkin would have been seriously put out by any such suggestion), though Woolf is a possible candidate. In fact, the theorists differ in their views as to whether *écriture féminine* can be produced by a man or not. Cixous argues that it can. But Irigaray, the psychoanalyst and thinker whose influence was paramount in the seventies, argues that it cannot. I want now to turn to the flamboyant work of Luce Irigaray, the most significant source of the French attempt to formulate an exclusively female language.

Irigaray

3.27 Luce Irigaray has always been a rebel. She began her career as a follower of Lacan. But her massive doctoral thesis, *Speculum de l'autre femme* ('Speculum of the other woman', 1974), resulted in her instant dismissal from Lacan's school – perhaps a propitious beginning for a woman who was to become a figurehead of feminism. Irigaray, unlike Kristeva, was not prepared to negotiate with patriarchy. Rather than the genderless semiotic flow existing within language that we find in Kristeva's thought, Irigaray suggests that a woman wishing to resist the symbolic order, as any woman who is not willing to repress her true femaleness must, will create a separate level of language, an *écriture féminine* to which men do not have access. Irigaray has little sympathy with Kristeva's insistence on gender as a matter of cultural positioning. Her celebration of women depends on their *biological* identity, which she sees as a gift rather than a curse. The women's writing she envisages will be a writing of the body – fluid, fertile and creative, not to be judged by the rules of patriarchy.

ACTIVITY

Given the assertive denial of logic in Irigaray's writing, it is well nigh impossible to summarize it coherently. The only way to form an idea of what Irigaray is saying, and, just as importantly, of how she is saying it, is to read for yourself. Here, then, is a sample of her writing – in fact, a famous, controversial and often quoted passage. Read it carefully, remembering that what you are reading is a valiant attempt to translate French of a kind that might well be described as untranslatable. After you have read the passage, ask yourself the following questions:

(a) How much does Irigaray's position here have in common with what you know of Kristeva's arguments?

(b) What seem to you to be the advantages for women, and the disadvantages, of Irigaray's point of view?

'She' is indefinitely other in herself. That is undoubtedly the reason she is called temperamental, incomprehensible, perturbed, capricious – not to mention her language in which 'she' goes off in all directions and in which 'he' is unable to discern the coherence of any meaning. Contradictory words seem a little crazy to the logic of reason, and inaudible for him who reads with ready-made grids, a code prepared in advance. In her statements – at least when she dares to speak out – woman retouches herself constantly. She just barely separates from herself some chatter, an exclamation, a half-secret, a sentence left in suspense – When she returns to it, it is only to set out again from another point of pleasure or pain. One must listen to her differently in order to hear an *'other meaning'* which is constantly in the process of weaving itself, at the same time ceaselessly embracing words and yet casting them off to avoid becoming fixed, immobilized. For when 'she' says something, it is already no longer identical to what she means. Moreover, her statements are never identical to anything. Their distinguishing feature is one of contiguity. They touch (*upon*). And when they wander too far from this nearness, she stops and begins again from 'zero': her body-sex organ.

It is therefore useless to trap women into giving an exact confession of what they mean, to make them repeat (themselves) so the meaning will be clear. They are already elsewhere than in this discursive machinery where you claim to take them by surprise. They have turned back within themselves, which does not mean the same thing as 'within yourself'. They do not experience the same interiority that you do and which perhaps you mistakenly presume they share. 'Within themselves' means *in the privacy of this silent, multiple, diffuse tact.* If you ask them insistently what they are thinking about, they can only reply: nothing. Everything.

(Marks and de Courtivron, 1981, p.103; from *Ce sexe qui n'en est pas un* – 'This sex which is not one' – 1977. Note the characteristic pun in the title, which means both 'This sex which is seen as merely negative, not a sex at all', and 'this sex which is not single, but multiple'.)

DISCUSSION

(a) Irigaray's claim that there is a firm identification between non-symbolic discourse and the female sex is one thing that she does *not* have in common with Kristeva. The opposition between 'she' and 'he' is the basis of this deliberately provocative and challenging extract. The association between women's language and the body, which is implied in Kristeva, is here directly stressed. Women's words seem to be a matter of touch, rooted in a physical identity. In Irigaray's terms, the quality of 'tact', traditionally assigned to women, reaffirms its origins in the Latin word for 'touch'.

Despite these differences of emphasis, what Irigaray is saying about women's language here is easily comparable with Kristeva's thoughts on the semiotic. There is a similar suspicion of definition, of single meanings attaching themselves to single words. Irigaray's language flows and floats, will not be tied down. It includes silence.

But in looking for Kristeva's shaping presence here, you might well have noticed the traces of another influence in Irigaray's thought. Did the first sentence of the passage strike a familiar note? '"She" is indefinitely other in herself.' It was, after all, de Beauvoir who had first pointed to women's identification with the 'other'. Irigaray's emphasis, however, is crucially different. What de Beauvoir had lamented as a handicap, Irigaray eulogizes as a strength.

(b) The attraction of Irigaray's polemical rhapsody seems to me to lie in this ebullient sense of confidence. She is prepared to overturn the most fundamental assumptions about what we should value in language and thought. She is not apologetic, defensive or self-pitying, and she calls everything into question. The intellectual appeal of a thinker who is prepared to take irreverence to quite such lengths is not to be underestimated. Nevertheless, the problems she raises are surely considerable. What did you think? We're really going back here to that central debate we raised in the opening section of the block – whether women should claim their right to an equal share in masculine privilege, or whether they ought to leave patriarchy to play its own games, and create a world of language for themselves. Irigaray makes spirited claims for the second, separatist position. But can women afford to leave the discourses of logic entirely in the hands of men? What would the political and economic effects of such a withdrawal be? Irigaray has argued that revolution will come about only through language. Can women afford to wait for that utopian millenium? While they are waiting, thinking women have to make their way in the world. How do you think most tutors would react if a student were to present a TMA along Irigarayan lines? Isn't Irigaray playing into the hands of the very forces she wishes to attack? Women are contradictory, illogical, there's no telling what they are talking about ... After all, that is exactly what the voices of patriarchy have been saying for years.

3.28 Irigaray feels no responsibility towards the welfare of those who seek to study within institutions which she would regard as hopelessly compromised by their position within the established masculine order. The implications of her theory seem to amount to a repudiation of direct feminist work for change. This has been the grounds of the resistance to such theory and for the reaction against it – which has always been strong in North America, less so in Britain.

Cixous

3.29 Not every French thinker, however, has been prepared to mark out the specifically female territory for *écriture féminine* that we find in the work of Irigaray. Hélène Cixous, the theorist, dramatist, poet and novelist whose thought I want to look at now, has taken quite a different approach. Her argument is that the qualities which distinguish *écriture féminine* may sometimes be possessed by male authors (she cites James Joyce and Jean Genet among her examples), though the cultural circumstances which have led to women's oppression make it more likely that they will be found in female writers. Cixous's published work, dating from 1968, hasn't been static. Her views on a number of significant matters have changed over the years. But she has always shown herself to be more prepared to engage with the worlds of history and politics than Irigaray, though she does so within the terms of an overall argument that is closely related to Irigaray's.

ACTIVITY

At this point, I want to give you the opportunity to judge Hélène Cixous's writing for yourself. You will find part of her 'The laugh of the Medusa' reproduced in the Reader (pp.316–26). Read it now, remembering that here again you are encountering a translation of a very idiosyncratic French original. As you read, keep the following questions in mind:

(a) What are the most important points of comparison between Cixous's position and those of Kristeva and Irigaray?

(b) Do you see anything in this essay that would incline you to accept my claim that Cixous demonstrates a readiness to engage with history and politics?

DISCUSSION

(a) Cixous's writing is crowded with ideas and, like all French feminist theory, it is by no means easy to summarize. The nature of this difficulty is in itself, it seems to me, the most significant way in which Cixous's work touches that of Kristeva and Irigaray. She too is concerned to question and challenge the patterns within which academic, or indeed political, arguments have conventionally been presented. The debate cannot be separated from the rhapsodic, circling language within which it is expressed.

The visionary, even mystic, intensity with which Cixous invokes her Utopia is a deliberate denial of the primacy of logic. Here Cixous is particularly close to Irigaray. Other points of comparison will have suggested themselves to you. Cixous, too, asserts that women's writing has a direct relationship with the body. She claims it as a celebration of fertility and life, 'undoing the work of death'. Her image of Medusa transforms the Greek myth, for this Medusa no longer freezes to stone all who encounter her. She is, after all, a liberating energy, perpetually laughing. But such laughter is not only an expression of '*jouissance*'. It may also be a threat – as Kate Millett, in a very different way, had shown. Laughter is potentially a powerfully subversive force. Annie Leclerc, a philosopher and novelist closely associated with Cixous, put the point succinctly:

> One must not wage war on man. That is his way of attaining value. Deny in order to affirm. Kill to love. One must simply deflate his values with the needle of ridicule.
>
> (in Marks and de Courtivron, 1981, p.79)

Cixous and her followers, like Irigaray, are exuberantly confident, positive and iconoclastic. After the forbidding tracts of Derrida and Lacan, such writing seemed invigorating indeed.

(b) I wonder what you felt about the question of Cixous's engagement – or disengagement – with the world of history and politics? There seem to me a number of points at which she does demonstrate an undeniably political inclination, one which invariably focuses on those she sees as silenced and dispossessed. In urging women to write, for instance, she talks about the mechanisms of publication as 'the imbecilic capitalist machinery, in which publishing houses are the crafty relayers of imperatives handed down by an economy that works against us and off our backs'. She also pays brief homage to a Woolfian concept of literary history: 'It is well known that the number of women writers (while having increased very slightly from the nineteenth century on) has always been ridiculously small.' More interesting still is the identification she claims between the oppressions of gender and the oppressions of race. To be female is to be black:

> You can incarcerate them, slow them down, get away with the old Apartheid routine, but for a time only. As soon as they begin to speak, at the same time as they're taught their name, they can be taught that their territory is black: because you are Africa, you are black. Your continent is dark. Dark is dangerous.

This notion is not unique to Cixous. As is so often the case, it may be traced back to de Beauvoir. It became a prevalent image: the MLF song *Debout les femmes!* has the line 'Nous sommes le continent noir' ('We are the dark continent'). In its sympathy with this idea, the French tradition shows itself to be sensitive to what has been said in the USA, for the growth of North American feminism is deeply rooted in the American civil rights movement of the sixties. (We will be returning to this point in our reading of Toni Morrison's *Song of Solomon*.) Similarly, Cixous recalls the American claim that feminism cannot be separate from the gay liberation movement: 'The Americans remind us, "We are all Lesbians".' Again, this is a point we shall come back to in our consideration of the poetry of Adrienne Rich.

Is it useful to underscore these associations – perhaps even inspiring? Or is Cixous just conjuring with words, retreating behind them, making *écriture féminine* a grandiosely specious substitute for political responsibility?

3.30 Whatever your feelings on these questions, we should note that Cixous has gone on to assert that they are central to the ways in which we might approach literature. She has founded a research seminar dedicated to finding a new structure for literary study, one without the individualistic competitiveness that she sees as a paralysing constraint on the conventions of academic scholarship. Members of her seminar attempt to work collectively, moving towards a fuller understanding of literary texts and issues. Cixous explains:

> We work together. In one of the oldest texts of the world – the Sumerian epic of Gilgamesh – Gilgamesh and Enkidu set out together to discover the secret of life and death. Throughout the text there is a rhyme like a refrain: 'alone I can do nothing but together we can do anything.' It might seem a platitude, but it's the oldest literary inscription of the world. It's 'give me your hand so that I may go and discover the secret of life and death'. I desire that hand.
>
> (quoted in Sellers, 1988, p.141)

A bizarre leftover from a sixties commune – or a genuinely new way to study literature? Or perhaps something of both? As always, Cixous's position is not easily pinned down. Elsewhere in the interview from which I have just quoted, she talks about the pressures of history. Her focus is still on language, and she is still thinking about women's capacity to find new languages. But here she shows that the concerns of language and gender have led her beyond separatism:

> History gives us lessons. The texts of Mandelstam, Celan, all those who were involved in violent political conflict, who were imprisoned in the concentration camps, are bearers of texts, suffering, heavy, impregnated with political reality.
>
> But I don't believe we can play with the facts. Someone who has not been in a concentration camp cannot say what someone who has been imprisoned says. But one thing we who have escaped the camps can do is to make the effort to turn our thoughts towards those who have been in captivity. The other thing is to try to find a language that corresponds to the reality of the camps.
>
> This is a question which has haunted me. In every one of my texts, through the troubles in Vietnam, Iran, the USSR – the list is endless – my question has been: how can we talk about it? Can we talk about it? Who has the

right to talk about it? What form must our talking about it take? What form can we give to our outrage, speaking about these things which are unspeakable, which take away our breath?

(Ibid., pp.151–2)

3.31 In quoting this passage, I am beginning to touch on the territory of the next block in the course, which is concerned with literature and history. But the course team's decision to juxtapose language and gender with literature and history was a deliberate one. As feminism continues to change and grow, their concerns look less and less separate.

4 Virginia Woolf: 'Kew Gardens'

4.1 In the first two blocks of the course, you thought about 'Kew Gardens' (1919) from the point of view of its narrative structure (in Block 1 Section 1 and Block 2 Section 3). You might find it helpful to remind yourself of your first response to the story at this point. In this section, we will be looking again at 'Kew Gardens', this time from a different viewpoint. Do the theories of language and gender discussed in the block help us to understand what happens in Virginia Woolf's story?

ACTIVITY

Re-read 'Kew Gardens' carefully. As you do so, you may find yourself noticing many things that did not strike you on your first reading. For the moment, I would like you to concentrate on the following questions:

(a) Why do you think Virginia Woolf chose to place her story in Kew Gardens?

(b) What do you notice about the language of the conversations between the people passing through the gardens?

DISCUSSION

(a) In thinking about the question of the story's setting, I wonder whether you find yourself recalling your work on *Mrs Dalloway*? The sense of a formally cultivated public space, where different kinds of people might randomly encounter each other, is important in that novel (published in 1925, remember, six years later than 'Kew Gardens'). Clarissa's meeting with Hugh Whitbread in the park (p.7) comes to mind here, or the different ways in which Peter Walsh and Maisie Johnson react when they happen upon the misery of Rezia and Septimus in Regent's Park (pp.25, 64). A similar sense of the chance meetings of isolated individuals lies behind Clarissa's party. But there the meetings take place within a particular social setting, largely controlled by Clarissa. And the party takes place in a house. One of the main reasons for setting this story in a garden, it seems to me, is that it allows Woolf to juxtapose the haphazard vitality of human life with that of nature.

Nature, yes: but nature of a certain kind. Would you agree that what 'Kew Gardens' gives us is a defamiliarized vision of the natural world: nature made strange, with an almost tropical vitality? As in *Mrs Dalloway*, flowers figure prominently. But they are exotic flowers, scarcely

English. Here they differ from the blooms of *Mrs Dalloway*, which were lovingly particularized details of an English context: 'delphiniums, sweet peas, bunches of lilac; and carnations, masses of carnations. There were roses; there were irises...' Compare those comfortingly familiar names with what is described in the opening paragraph of 'Kew Gardens': plants 'unfurling at the tip red or blue or yellow petals marked with spots of colour raised upon the surface; and from the red, blue, or yellow gloom of the throat emerged a straight bar, rough with gold dust and slightly clubbed at the end'. It is impossible, I would say, to name those flowers; they have become intense sensory impressions, divorced from the classifications we use to order and perhaps to humanize or control the energy of the natural world. One of the sources of power in Lawrence's gipsy, you'll remember, is his namelessness.

Is there something disturbing about these unnamed flowers? Words such as 'gloom', 'rough', 'slightly clubbed' are not, after all, usually associated with floral imagery. Did you find them sinister? You might well have done. But they are not, surely, threatening in any active way. They are safely contained within their 'oval-shaped flower-bed' and are as much a product of civilization as Clarissa's drawing room. Trissie, it is true, remembers 'orchids and cranes among wild flowers, a Chinese pagoda and a crimson-crested bird'. But these flowers are certainly not wild in the way they might be in a Georgian poem of the same period (as, for instance, the willow-herb and meadowsweet are evocatively and anciently wild in Edward Thomas's 'Adlestrop', 1915). Trissie's memory sounds more like a pattern on a plate than a vision of unchanging nature. Kew Gardens is seen as part of a city, an expression of a civilization that Virginia Woolf's writing makes foreign but never anything but urban. The word 'Chinese' recurs in the final sentence of the story, where London is described:

> Like a vast nest of Chinese boxes all of wrought steel turning ceaselessly one within the other the city murmured; on the top of which the voices cried aloud and the petals of myriads of flowers flashed their petals in the air.

To allude to China introduces a resonance of the alien. But the civilization of China was held to be delicate, highly cultured – fastidiously aloof from the primitive Oriental passion that might be suggested in those voices crying aloud. To choose Kew Gardens as a setting was a particularly appropriate way of suggesting this quality of a refined foreignness in the apparently mundane context of London, since Kew is famed for its collection of rare and curious plants assembled from all corners of the world.

(b) What did you notice about the conversations between the four groups of characters assembled in this vivid setting? The first thing that strikes me is that there is a sense in which they can hardly be regarded as conversations at all. The first three, at least, seem to have only the most oblique connection with the language that most people actually use, or have ever used, when they talk to each other. Simon and Eleanor's words are an odd mixture of unspoken thought and memory (the dragon-fly, the kiss) and everyday speech ('Tell me, Eleanor, d'you ever think of the past?'). The language of William and his charge might seem more straightforward, if it were not so evident that the old man is mad: 'murmuring about the forests of Uruguay blanketed with the wax petals of tropical roses, nightingales, sea beaches, mermaids and women drowned at sea...' The 'two elderly women of the lower middle class' are not at all mad, with their stubbornly repetitive gossip about family affairs and groceries. But we are given their complicated dialogue as a rhythmical chant, divorced from their practical preoccupations:

> 'Sugar, flour, kippers, greens
> Sugar, sugar, sugar.'

The only speech that is realistically rendered is that between Trissie and her lover. Yet their words are explicitly said to be incapable of expressing their meaning: 'words with short wings for their heavy body of meaning, inadequate to carry them far.' Throughout the story what people mean and what they actually say are shown to be distinct. Like the plants and insects which surround them, these men and women are seen to be uncertain, hardly rational, as they straggle past the flowers 'with a curiously irregular movement not unlike that of the white and blue butterflies who crossed the turf in zig-zag flights from bed to bed'.

Indeed, the only creature in the story who is seen behaving in a thoroughly sensible and logical way is the snail, with his apparently 'definite goal' from which nothing diverts him. ('The snail had now considered every possible method of reaching his goal without going round the dead leaf or climbing over it. Let alone the effort needed for climbing a leaf, he was doubtful whether the thin texture which vibrated with such an alarming crackle when touched even by the tip of his horns would bear his weight; and this determined him finally to creep beneath it...') If people are as capricious as butterflies, a snail, it seems, can still behave with firm good sense.

4.2 What has all this got to do with language and gender? I've postponed the question in the hope that you will have begun to answer it for yourself. Did it strike you, for instance, that the snail's limited perspective and dogged determination make him a very male mollusc in Virginia Woolf's terms? A humbler version of the clammy Hugh Whitbread (perhaps his prototype?), he would, if promoted to humanity, have been well able to help Lady Bruton with her letters to *The Times*. But the snail is of course partly a joke. What more serious points might be made?

4.3 It seems clear that this story is related to Virginia Woolf's thoughtful questioning of what she perceived as male qualities in logic, language and literature. 'Kew Gardens' could, from this perspective, be seen as a feminist statement. In some ways, it might be said that it is a more extreme act of fictional defiance than *Mrs Dalloway*, for here Virginia Woolf dispenses altogether with anything that might be described as a coherent plot, constructing instead a narrative of apparently unconnected fragments. You'll recall that Graham Martin comments on this aspect of 'Kew Gardens' in Block 1. Here 'story' takes second place to 'discourse' – to an extent that makes 'story' scarcely appropriate as a term for what is attempted. As Dennis Walder pointed out, 'Kew Gardens' is 'a far cry from the "conventional" or "traditional" narrative in which we typically follow a character or group of characters forward through time towards a final twist or climax' (Block 2, paragraph 3.8). Might this innovatory quality, then, be seen as an attack on the symbolic order? Does it make the story an example of *écriture féminine*? Woolf's writing has in fact attracted a good deal of attention from feminist theorists. Here's Kristeva, quoted from an interview:

> In women's writing, language seems to be seen from a foreign land; is it seen from the point of view of an asymbolic, spastic body? Virginia Woolf describes suspended states, subtle sensations and, above all, colours – green, blue –, but she does not dissect language as Joyce does. Estranged from language, women are visionaries, dancers who suffer as they speak.
>
> (in Gauthier, 1974)

4.4 The quality of alienation and strangeness that Kristeva points to as a general feature of Woolf's language is one that we have noticed as a prominent feature of 'Kew Gardens', where language does indeed sometimes seem 'to be seen from a foreign land'. An emphasis on colour and sensation, a spasmodic structure, perhaps also a visionary aspiration in the final paragraph, might all be claimed for the story. In these ways Kristeva's citing of Woolf as a source of 'women's writing' seems to be helpful.

4.5 What has Kristeva left out? My own feeling (and you might well want to disagree) would be that she gives rather a negative impression of what Woolf is trying to do. I would argue that Kristeva's emphasis on alienation and suffering needs to be qualified in this case by an idea that is elsewhere central to her thought: the idea of joy. The voices in 'Kew Gardens' might speak of uncertainty, memory or loss, but they do so with 'such depth of contentment, such passion of desire, or, in the voices of the children, such freshness of surprise' that the impression they leave cannot altogether be one of distress. 'Kew Gardens' strikes me as an act of celebration, rather than an expression of suffering.

4.6 The story may well be understood, as Kristeva suggests, as a dance. But Kristeva's reference to colour is important too, for the story might also be seen as a picture. 'Yellow and black, pink and snow white, shapes of all these colours, men, women, and children, were spotted for a second on the horizon, and then, seeing the breadth of colour that lay upon the grass, they wavered and sought shade beneath the trees, dissolving like drops of water in the yellow and green atmosphere, staining it faintly with red and blue.' 'Kew Gardens' represents Virginia Woolf's most committed attempt to break free from the linearity of narrative and write with the visual immediacy of a painter. In 1918, while working on the story, she was close to her sister, the artist Vanessa Bell. They were thinking about the possible interaction between painting and writing. The result – the first appearance of 'Kew Gardens' in 1919, as a pamphlet issued by the Hogarth Press – was something close to a collaboration. Vanessa Bell provided two woodcuts, a frontispiece illustrating the conversation of the two elderly women, and a smaller tailpiece depicting a caterpillar and a butterfly. In the frontispiece, the human figures and the flowers are not distinct – they flow into one pattern, as they do in the text. Word and image become part of a whole.

4.7 If there is women's writing, is there also women's painting? That is a question that we can't begin to answer here. But the creative association between Vanessa Bell and Virginia Woolf is indispensable to what is attempted in 'Kew Gardens'. It reminds us that Virginia Woolf did not work in a cultural vacuum, locked in her own imagination. She was alert to what was happening around her. She learned from others – especially from other women. If 'Kew Gardens' can be read as an *example* of *écriture féminine*, it also takes its place in the *construction* of women's history.

5 *Ernest Hemingway: 'The Short Happy Life Of Francis Macomber'*

5.1 Ernest Hemingway was born in 1899 in Illinois, one of six children in a prosperous family. His mother was a highly cultured woman; his father (a doctor) preferred hunting and fishing. He became a reporter, and – because of deficient eyesight – an ambulance driver when the United States entered the

First World War in 1918. He was wounded, and decorated for saving a man more severely wounded than himself.

5.2 In 1920 he married a wealthy woman and moved with her to Paris, living an extravagant life in the company of other expatriate writers such as Gertrude Stein, Ezra Pound and F. Scott Fitzgerald. He began to publish stories; his first novel *The Sun Also Rises* (1926), about a man made impotent by his war wounds, established his typically sparse and concrete style. In *A Farewell to Arms* (1929) the relationship between the American Army officer and the British nurse is an archetype of literary machismo and feminine submission. Increasingly, his work glorified – even created – a cult of tough, laconic masculinism in which war, and war-substitutes such as big-game hunting and bull-fighting, were seen as superior activities because they excluded women.

5.3 He himself became a cult-figure. He was a war-correspondent in Spain and during the Second World War, but recently more sceptical research has suggested that not all the hair-raising stories he filed then were founded in personal experience. He hunted, travelled and drank on the same 'heroic' scale, and he also came to regard writing as an heroic activity, in which the writer contended with the threats of money, sex and fame. He committed suicide in 1961.

5.4 'The Short Happy Life of Francis Macomber' was written in 1936, and reprinted in 1939 as the first of *The First Forty-nine Stories*. A short preface begins: 'There is not much to say about these stories' – but there is. The preface itself provides examples of how eloquently omissions can speak:

> ...Madrid was always a good place for working. So was Paris, and so were Key West, Florida, in the cool months; the ranch, near Cooke City, Montana; Kansas City; Chicago; Toronto, and Havana, Cuba.

How does that make you feel, slogging away in Barnsley or Surbiton? Following, and set out in a paragraph on its own, is the statement:

> Some other places were not so good, but maybe we were not so good when we were in them.

– without any amplification, or any explanation. What is meant by 'not so good'? Not for a moment do you assume that it was merely difficult to buy typewriter ribbons. You assume something much more serious, indeed something on an heroic or tragic scale and, what's more, some exotic hazard to which the artist is peculiarly liable. Paradoxically, if he had continued, and said 'I was drinking too much', the effect would be diminished. He is actually able to say more by saying less, rather in the way that something described as 'unspeakable' signifies something much more dreadful than anything we can think of. This pared-down, laconic style is equally familiar from films of the same period, or the war years that followed. Humphrey Bogart in *Casablanca* conveys how inexpressibly powerful his feelings are by registering next to nothing in his face and voice. Thus, understatement that verges on silence has come to signify a certain kind of masculinity.

5.5 In a previous section of this block you will have addressed the question of whether men and women express themselves in different languages, and whether women writers should actively pursue a language different from the prevailing, patriarchal norm. As you will have seen, the norm, the neutral and the masculine have traditionally been elided. But in Hemingway we can see the construction of a specifically masculine language, and as we have already seen in the preceding discussion, one in which silence becomes signification. The point will not be new to you. In Block 4, you'll remember, part of the ideological content of *A Sahibs' War* lay in the text's silence in certain respects. We have also considered Lawrence's 'virginal' silence. But in the previous theoretical section of this block we have been looking at silence in relation to *women's* utterance. What follows should enable you to debate the issue more extensively by suggesting that when silence is gendered it is not always female.

ACTIVITY

Read Hemingway's story (Prose Anthology pp. 84–113) before proceeding, looking out for its silences and understatements, for the ways in which the inner and outer lives of its characters are presented, and how male stereotypes are constructed.

5.6 The three main characters are the big white (British) hunter, the failed (American) macho man, and the American beauty. And, you might have added, the lion. I wonder if you noticed that while Hemingway feels entitled to describe the thoughts of Macomber, the white hunter and the lion, he does not give us those of Mrs Macomber. Women, it is implied, are unfathomable, perhaps unintelligible. We see her from the outside; we are told what she sees, and what Wilson supposes her to be thinking; but we are given practically nothing of what she actually thinks or feels from within – and absolutely nothing during the crucial final paragraphs. Male critics, however, appear not to have noticed this omission, and have felt free to lavish their own interpretations on what is in fact a very minimal treatment by the author. In *Ernest Hemingway: the pursuit of heroism* (1968), Leo Gurko claims in a feat of creative interpretation that '[Macomber's] cowardice secretly gratifies his wife, and she proceeds to betray him'. It is, he continues, because she is 'unable to bear the prospect of her husband's bravery' that she shoots him. Gurko is not the only one of Hemingway's critics who seems to have felt impelled to outdo him:

> In addition to shooting her husband, which she does in a sort of Freudian accident, meant, as it were, but not consciously worked out, the beautiful Mrs Francis Macomber had investigated him, found out his weaknesses, and used them as weapons to hunt and master him. It is only when she knows that her mastery has been lost that she pulls the fatal trigger.
>
> (Pearsall, 1973, p.198)

Did you notice in that last example how Mrs Macomber has been rendered unconscious – the state in which women are most dangerous? Both these over-readings miss the point, which is Hemingway's silence. The consciousness of a lion, he implies, is more accessible to a man than that of a woman.

5.7 The authorial silence that surrounds Margot includes a silence which makes her more desirable in Wilson's eyes. He is so much the archetypal strong silent type that I wonder if you found him rather laughable? Carlos Baker did not. He called Wilson 'the man free of women and of fear … the standard of manhood towards which Macomber rises' (Benson, 1975, p.47).

5.8 But another essay in the same collection makes a valiant attempt to see Wilson, far more critically, as a satire on British imperialism and a travesty of machismo values. Virgil Hutton claims that 'through [his] mechanical harping on what is supposed to be good form, Hemingway satirizes the Britisher's respect for decorum'. He cites the passage in which Margot says (without even an adverb to describe how she said it) 'I didn't know you were allowed to shoot them from cars'. Wilson corrects her 'coldly'. The 'buff' (it is part of his 'silence' to shorten or omit words whenever he can) were only *followed* in the car. But having disposed of the suggestion that it might have been unsporting, he goes on to pile on the machismo by adding that it was really more dangerous and – most thrilling of all – illegal. When he then says that 'if they heard about it in Nairobi' he would 'lose his licence for one thing', there is surely more of bravado than confession about it. Do you think Hemingway is critical of Wilson's attitudes? Look carefully at the text.

5.9 I can't find any evidence myself, but that of course does not mean that as a reader I have no right to find Wilson loathsome. Even though the text contains no ostensible marks of disapproval, it displays Wilson as a reprehensible travesty. Look at another example. Wilson admits to threatening his servants with 'fifteen of the best'. Again the tone of Macomber's response is not identified: '"It's quite legal," Wilson said. "You're supposed to fine them."' Well, is it legal or isn't it? He turns the issue into a rhetorical question: "Which would you rather do? Take a good birching or lose your pay?" The implied answer seems to be 'take it like a man'. And of course no one – not even the narrator – thinks of asking the servants themselves.

5.10 How might we know if Hemingway wanted his readers to disapprove of Wilson without him saying so very explicitly? One technique would be to make sure that the descriptions of the man made his appearance physically repellent (remember Angus Calder's discussion of Sandy Stranger's 'piggy eyes'?). Naturalistic descriptions are frequently presented in a narrative as if they were 'unauthored', and they ask to be specially scrutinized in a text that is apparently being kept free from authorial opinions or presence. Virgil Hutton draws attention to Wilson's red face – 'an unusual mark for a hero' – and sees it as the red of the British Empire on the map. In fact, in the paragraph that describes Wilson, Hemingway draws attention to the red, the white and the blue. But these are the colours of the Stars and Stripes as well as the Union Jack. In a hero of this kidney, having a face like a flag is hardly undermining. Hutton also draws attention to Wilson's 'machine gunner's eyes', but although that would not be a sign of approval in my book, it might well be in Hemingway's.

ACTIVITY

In the previous theoretical sections you considered the notion of *écriture féminine*. Now, an aggressively virile writer such as Hemingway offers us an opportunity to try to identify an explicitly masculine language. As I suggested earlier, silence, or near silence, is a salient characteristic of his idiom. So look through the story and make a note of Wilson's 'silences' and what they signify. For example, he says, 'I say, you wouldn't like to drop my beauty as a topic, would you?'. A man's appearance is not a proper subject for discussion; but Margot's (diminishing) beauty is one of her most significant attributes. It is she, of course, who has drawn attention to his looks: women are superficial, we are being told, only interested in appearance.

DISCUSSION

I'm sure you noticed that Wilson's speech is characterized by omissions:

> Hundred's about right. Might have to take him a bit under. Shouldn't chance a shot at much over that.

And that he calls buffalo 'buff', thus diminishing the creature and confirming his membership of an élite with its own lingo. In contrast, he despises the anthropomorphic whimsy of the amateurs, who refer to lions and elephants as 'Old Simba' and 'Tembo'.

When Margot (vividly) describes the eland served for lunch as 'the big cowy things that jump like hares', Wilson says tersely, 'I suppose that describes them'. 'Cowy' and 'hares' are words too tame and domestic for his approval. The narrator, too, repudiates such homely epithets when describing the animals: the bulls are 'like big black tank cars'. Huge sectors of reference are taboo; it is perhaps when the occasional references to the forbidden dimensions creep in that we most notice what is missing:

> In the orchard bush they found a herd of impala, and leaving the car they stalked one old ram with long, widespread horns and Macomber killed it with a very creditable shot that knocked the buck down at a good two hundred yards and sent the herd off bounding wildly and leaping over one another's backs in long, leg-drawn-up leaps as *unbelievable and as floating as those one makes sometimes in dreams.*
>
> (p.90)

That 'one' seems to belong to a different world. Wilson has very little in the way of a subconscious, and his access to the lyrical is strictly limited. But even what he does know at the subconscious level, he refuses to articulate. We are given, you'll remember, a bravura account of the wounded lion's sensations. Macomber 'did not know how the lion had felt' – he lacks the hunter's empathy with his prey; Wilson, on the other hand, 'knew something about it and only expressed it by saying, "Damned fine lion"'.

This is what is 'wrong' with Francis Macomber. Though he does not know the 'right' things, he says too much, and he speaks the unsayable. He does not even know that he is not supposed to talk about his failure to stand his ground when the lion charges. In essence, Wilson despises him because he talks and thinks too much. Macomber does not know that the proper manly (and gentlemanly) conduct includes saying nothing. The relationship between the manly and the gentlemanly is tense and inconsistent: pursuing game from a vehicle rather than on foot may be caddish, but let a woman question it and threatened virility will outflank the suggestion. Wilson is the arbiter of right thinking, consistent or not. He is insulted when Macomber gaffes by asking if 'it [his failure] ... will go any further?': 'It's supposed to be bad form to ask us not to talk...' A silence within a silence is the ideal. And not to know this renders Macomber 'a bloody four-letter man' – presumably something excremental or female. Even Wilson's thoughts impose a silence upon him. His mind prefers the euphemism, part of the same elliptical code among the white hunters in which the phrase 'I'm still drinking their whisky' can be rendered only as 'everything has gone to pot', which is yet another understated code phrase, signifying a complaint that it would somehow be indecent to articulate. Even euphemisms are only translatable into other euphemisms. The truth remains unsayable.

When even Wilson's need to express his feelings becomes unavoidable, he is forced to resort to the elaborate strategy of quoting Shakespeare. You may have felt at that moment that it is really the narrator who is trying to avoid expressing fine sentiments on his own behalf. Quoting Shakespeare is one way of putting a distance between feeling and its expression, but even so Wilson is 'embarrassed, having brought out this thing he had lived by'. *Thing?* Perhaps a thing is more manly than a feeling: '...he had seen men come of age before and it always moved him. It was not a matter of their twenty-first birthday.' Macomber, it seems, had experienced a *rite de passage*. But he still does not know when to be silent:

> 'Do you have that feeling of happiness about what's going to happen?' Macomber asked, still exploring his new wealth.
>
> 'You're not supposed to mention it,' Wilson said... 'Much more fashionable to say you're scared ... Doesn't do to talk too much about all this. Talk the whole thing away. No pleasure in anything if you mouth it up too much.'

> 'You're both talking rot,' said Margot. 'Just because you've chased some helpless animals in a motor car you talk like heroes.'
>
> (p.110)

At this point the narrative might seem to contain its own critique. But Margot's belittling (or objective?) gloss on the men's language is undercut by Wilson's interpretation: 'She's worried about it already, he thought.' In his eyes, anxiety is her only possible motivation for this reaction to the way in which she has been excluded from the newly-shared language of the men.

5.11 If Hemingway identified the masculine with silence, then by extension perhaps he associated articulation, particularly about feelings, with the feminine; and perhaps hence felt that to be a writer was to jeopardize his own virility and allow himself to be compromised by female garrulity.

5.12 By now you may either be reeling or revelling in the free play of contradictions. Adrienne Rich, Cora Kaplan, Luce Irigaray (among many others) have claimed that silence is both a condition of women's oppression and a part of their language. But Hemingway has staked a counterclaim in the same territory. (You might add that Wilson is as averse to logic as Irigaray!) Yet it is not quite the same silence: Hemingway's male silence is paradoxically articulate, and it is not an oppression. Wilson's silence is the self-claimed right of a superior being not to explain itself.

5.13 If writing is itself a feminine activity, then elaboration and natural description may be areas in which the macho writer is particularly vulnerable. You may have noticed passages which seem deliberately to flout literary conventions. Look at the repeated 'ands' in the following:

> But the other bull was moving steadily at the same gallop and he missed, throwing a spout of dirt, and Wilson missed and the dust rose in a cloud and Wilson shouted, 'Come on. He's too far!' and grabbed his arm and they were in the car again…
>
> (p.105)

Not copy-book style – though of course the effect is achieved by means of a language that draws attention to itself, and that, as we have frequently seen, is a characteristic of the 'literary'. But in this case the defiance of conventional practice is an act of literary machismo, which apparently repudiates elegance or refinement or any other drawing-room characteristics.

5.14 The most striking discrepancy in Hemingway's style is between the deliberately fragmented, inchoate appraisal of what goes on inside Wilson's head and the unerringly fluent descriptions of the natural world. I've already drawn your attention to the description of the impala. But do not make the mistake of thinking that the physical vividness of such writing is gender-neutral. Remember that the buffalo are 'like big black tank cars'. Search the epithets in any descriptive passage carefully and you will find that they refer mostly to mass and form, and that any more lyrical or quasi-'feminine' notes are excluded. What's more, all the animals are male, and their horns, where the species has them, are particularly important. Even the more or less incidental impala is 'an old ram with long, widespread horns'. One of the buffalo has 'close to a fifty-inch spread'. And look at the poor lion, with his 'dark mane … huge … his shoulders heavy, his barrel of a body bulking smoothly'. The description of his wounding is such a *tour de force* that we may confuse it with objectivity. But the salient phrases all come from one side of the gender line: 'majestically … coolly … not afraid … cracking crash … a slam of a .30-06 220-grain solid bullet … sudden hot scalding nausea…' In the midst of the carnage we are expected to register, and presumably respect, the precise calibre of the bullet. Re-read the paragraph yourself and I think you will identify the aesthetics of the war-movie.

5.15 But all this male expertise and empathy is rather undermined when Wilson, referring to the lion's hunt, speaks of '*his* kill'. It's actually *lionesses* that do the killing for the family group.

5.16 There is no space here to pursue every aspect of this challenging story. I want to conclude by suggesting in more general terms some of the ways in which, retrospectively, you might include it in your thinking about other issues spanning the course. I suggested earlier that Lawrence's misogynistic change of heart was partly a reaction to post-war male anxiety. Hemingway's anxiety seems to have been chronic, but like Lawrence he seems to have feared that his nation's manhood was imperilled. If you look at the lengthy description of Macomber you will notice that what is 'wrong' with him – according to the story's values – is that he reads too much, and is tolerant to a 'sinister' degree. Surely the ideal he falls short of is not merely macho but fascistic?

5.17 Like Lawrence, Hemingway had also lived abroad for much of his writing life and came to identify in the 'foreign' male a masculinity that was under threat among the males of his own kind. In Forster, too, you could say that sexuality is located in the 'foreign'. Is this a crisis of sexual or national identity? In all three cases the boundaries are further confused by class. Macomber is an *arriviste,* trying to learn what cannot be bought. You might well bring this story into any discussion of class, race or sex. Mrs Macomber is an American too, of course, and like Forster's Ango-Indians, deadlier than her male counterparts. Gender ideologies cannot be separated from any other deep-rooted prejudice in our perceptions of the world.

5.18 There has not been space here to draw your attention to the racial ideologies that constitute another effective silence in this story, but I'm sure you will have been aware of them. The largest part of the cast is excluded from the author's attention. None of the mess 'boys', gun-bearers, drivers, skinners, trackers or beaters ever emerge into speech. They are inaudible, invisible – and expendable:

> 'We lost a gun-bearer. Did you notice it?'
>
> 'My God, no,' Macomber said.
>
> 'Here he comes,' Wilson said. 'He's all right. He must have fallen off when we left the first bull.'
>
> (p.107)

Wilson is constantly barking at them 'in rapid Swahili', which is in effect an extension of his silence, since neither Macomber nor his wife understands it and what he says is not translated for the reader. Language here means power, both to command the Africans and to exclude the Macombers. Compare with these absences what we are told of the lion's thinking. We are given more of the guns' language than of the Africans': '*whunk ... ca-ra-wong ... carawong ... whunk*'. Well, all I can say is 'Kerpow'.

6 Gender and genre

6.1 The title of this section might well strike you as a puzzle. Why should there be any connection between gender and genre? And if there is – if, say, we should discover that the business of writing tragic plays has been predominantly a masculine concern – why should it matter?

6.2 Let's begin our exploration of these questions by thinking about literary reputation, an area where we might expect the cultural constructions of gender to be conspicuous. If you were asked to draw up a list of the most widely known women writers, who would you include? Jane Austen? George Eliot? The Brontë sisters? Virginia Woolf? Or, in more contemporary terms, perhaps you'd think of Iris Murdoch, or Doris Lessing? Maybe Barbara Cartland?

6.3 All the women I've mentioned are novelists. I'd be surprised if the first names that came into your head were those of dramatists. Though women – from Aphra Behn (1640–89), Joanna Baillie (1762–1851), to Caryl Churchill (b.1938) – have written successfully for the stage, they have not become household names. Did you think of any women poets? Sylvia Plath, perhaps, whose work will be discussed later in this block. Other poets may well have occurred to you. You might have thought of the ancient Greek poet Sappho, nineteenth-century writers such as Elizabeth Barrett Browning, Christina Rossetti, Emily Dickinson, or twentieth-century figures like Marianne Moore or Hilda Doolittle, whose 'Oread' you encountered in Block 2 Section 1. But as a general rule it does seem to have been in the field of fiction that women's role in the history of literature has been most fully recognized.

6.4 Of course, literary fame is not necessarily identical with the scale of literary production. Thousands of poems, novels or plays have been written and forgotten, or undervalued, or simply never published in any form. Many such lost texts were by women. Feminist scholars and publishers have done much to rewrite our sense of the literary past (see Section 1). As a result of their work, the achievements of women writers of all kinds are now more generously valued. But the very fact that these efforts were (and are) necessary, shows that gender has been closely bound up with the survival of literary prestige. And it remains true that academic histories of poetry, and still more those of drama, have rarely granted women the central place that they have established for themselves in the history of fiction. Our course is no exception to this general rule. You have, in the previous six blocks, studied a number of works of fiction by women (Doris Lessing's 'The Old Chief Mshlanga', Virginia Woolf's *Mrs Dalloway* and 'Kew Gardens', Flannery O'Connor's 'Revelation', Muriel Spark's *The Prime of Miss Jean Brodie*) – though they have been fewer in number than the novels and short stories by men that you have read. But there is no play by a woman on the course, and, up to this point, very few poems written by women ('Blackberrying' by Sylvia Plath, 'Oread' by Hilda Doolittle, 'The Farmer's Bride' by Charlotte Mew, and the poetry of Grace Nichols).

6.5 Why should women have found it so difficult to establish their presence in poetry and drama? Many reasons have been put forward. Before going on to look more closely at the relationship between gender and genre, I'd like to give some attention to one of the earliest and most influential contributions to the debate.

ACTIVITY

Please turn to the extract from Virginia Woolf's *A Room of One's Own* (1929) given in your Reader, and read the passage beginning 'Here am I asking why women did not write poetry...' as far as 'the length of the winter's night' (pp.77–9). You've already thought about the arguments Virginia Woolf sets out in this book in relation to language and gender (see Block 2 Section 4 and Section 1 of this block); now I want to consider her views about what has made it hard for women to make a recognized contribution to poetry and drama. What reasons does Virginia Woolf suggest here?

DISCUSSION

Woolf's historical speculations deal with the conditions of literary production in Elizabethan England, at a time when the development of prose fiction was in its earliest stages. Her argument conflates drama and poetry, the two genres that predominated in the period, for though she is talking primarily about the theatre, she is also concerned with the barriers that might have prevented women from becoming poets. Would you agree that she sees these barriers largely in social and economic terms? The imaginative life of Shakespeare's sister is comparable to that of her brother; she is 'as adventurous, as agog to see the world'; she has 'a gift like her brother's, for the tune of words. Like him, she has a taste for the theatre'. Or, if she differed from her brother, then only cultural circumstances were to blame – for how could genius have been born, 'among women whose work began, according to Professor Trevelyan, almost before they were out of the nursery, who were forced to it by their parents and held to it by all the power of law and custom?' Judith Shakespeare had neither money nor independence, and her education was rudimentary: 'She had no chance of learning grammar and logic, let alone of reading Horace and Virgil.' Given that the poetic traditions of the day were firmly based on the illustrious precedent of the classics, what chance had she of making her way as a poet?

She had still less hope of following her brother into the theatre. Virginia Woolf's argument draws attention to some of the most fundamental reasons for her exclusion. The theatre is a public place, and plays have generally concerned themselves with public action, while all but a very few women were firmly confined to the domestic sphere. Only with the Restoration in 1660 were women allowed to take parts on the public stage, and it was not until around that time that women first began to write for the commercial theatre (Aphra Behn's first play, *The Forced Marriage*, was written in 1670). A chaste woman could risk no association with the theatre, for reasons that Woolf makes clear enough:

> The manager – a fat, loose-lipped man – guffawed. He bellowed something about poodles dancing and women acting – no woman, he said, could possibly be an actress. He hinted – you can imagine what. She could get no training in her craft. Could she even seek her dinner in a tavern or roam the street at midnight?

Did you notice how the passage goes on? 'Yet her genius was for fiction and lusted to feed abundantly upon the lives of men and women and the study of their ways.' Woolf is here using the term 'fiction' in its broadest sense – story-telling, rather than novel-writing. Nevertheless, her comments here suggest her deepest convictions about the nature of women's literary creativity – and perhaps about men's too? It does not, she implies, lie in the formulation of transcendent truth, still less in the wish to teach, instruct, and reform. The proper food of Judith Shakespeare's blocked genius was the 'lives of men and women and the study of their ways'. Is Woolf hinting that the talents of Shakespeare's sister might have found their fullest expression in a genre that did not exist for her: the novel?

6.6 What Woolf had to say about the buried gifts of Judith Shakespeare has become a recurrent theme of feminist literary scholarship. In 1979, Sandra Gilbert and Susan Gubar (whose work was introduced in Section 1) recalled the theme in the title of an influential collection of essays on women's poetry in the twentieth century: *Shakespeare's Sisters*. Building on observations made by Woolf fifty years before, Gilbert and Gubar develop them in new directions.

ACTIVITY

You will find an extract from the introduction to this book reproduced in the Reader ('Women poets', pp.27–33). Please read it now.

(a) What seem to you the most important convictions held in common by Gilbert and Gubar and Woolf?

(b) In what ways does their thinking differ?

DISCUSSION

Like Woolf, Gilbert and Gubar suggest that the factors which have excluded women from poetry have been primarily external ones: the reaction of male readers, and the difficulties encountered by women seeking education, intellectual companionship and economic independence. Gilbert and Gubar take issue with the practical consequences of the 'masculinist' notion that the 'very nature of lyric poetry is inherently incompatible with the nature or essence of femaleness'. This is the assumption that permits the condescension and resentment that has marked the reactions (devastatingly quoted by Gilbert and Gubar) of so many male critics and reviewers to the work of women poets.

In considering why literary women should so often have opted for the novel rather than poetry, Gilbert and Gubar return to a question posed by both the life and writing of Virginia Woolf. What is the source of the association between women's writing and insanity? The imagined life of Judith Shakespeare ended in madness and suicide. Is the life of a woman poet always to be identified with suffering and instability? If so, are the frustrations and hindrances of a hostile culture to blame, or are there deeper reasons? This is a complex question, with implications that are not limited to women. After all, neither madness nor suicide is unknown among male poets. If Kristeva is right to suggest that the irrational drives of the semiotic are indispensable to the energies of poetic writing, perhaps all poets, male and female, are open to the damaging consequences of a deeply-held cultural suspicion of the subversions that poetry can represent.

Gilbert and Gubar's line of argument leads them to discuss some of the most fundamental differences between the practice of fiction and that of poetry. What did you make of the distinctions they claim? Would you agree, for instance, that the commercial potential of novel-writing has helped to give it a lower status in our culture? Or has it had the opposite effect?

In considering these and related questions, Gilbert and Gubar adopt an analytical tone which is very different from the sense of direct personal engagement communicated by Woolf's fictional account of the life and death of Judith Shakespeare. You might have noted this as the central distinction between their approach and that of Woolf. Gilbert and Gubar, for all their undoubted feminist commitment, are writing within the terms of professional academic prose – a well-defined model of writing in itself, quite distinct from that of the literary essay to which *A Room of One's Own* belongs. Supported with references to the work of other scholars, with footnotes, and a formally objective perspective, Gilbert and Gubar write as critics. Woolf's limited use of scholarly authority is largely ironic (the magisterial Professor Trevelyan, and the bishop: 'How much thinking those old gentlemen used to save one!'). She writes as a writer. In the first sentence of the extract from *A Room of One's Own* that we have just been thinking about, she roundly declares her own presence, her lack of scholarly authority: 'Here am I asking why women did not write poetry in the Elizabethan age, and I am not sure how they were educated...'

In the final paragraph of their article, Gilbert and Gubar consider the role of the writerly 'I'. Could this be the most insurmountable barrier between women and lyric poetry? Here women could be seen to be caught in the most subtle double bind of all. On the one hand, they are identified with subjectivity, with particularity and emotion. On the other hand, the aristocratic or even priestly implications in the powerful role of the poet deny women this culturally prestigious expression of inwardness. Women's identification with subjectivity has marked them as the appropriate subject-matter of poetry, while their entry into the discourse as authors has been made deeply problematic. Here, Gilbert and Gubar begin to explore an area present only by implication in Woolf's argument. Other critics, adopting a very different perspective from that of either Woolf or Gilbert and Gubar, have given sustained attention to the question of the construction of subjectivity within poetic discourse, and it is to this second line of approach that I now want to turn.

6.7 The arguments of Woolf and Gilbert and Gubar assume that the factors that have excluded women from the writing of poetry are fundamentally social and economic, that there is no deeper reason to prevent their becoming poets. But the growth of psychoanalytic theory has brought some of these assumptions into question. Though feminists interested in psychoanalysis have been ready to accept that such social and economic factors (women's limited education, their economic dependence on fathers and husbands) have indeed made it harder for them to succeed in the genre, they claim that the nature of women's access to language itself is the first and most significant impediment.

6.8 You will remember that Lacan's model for the acquisition of language turns on the idea that the child must enter into the 'symbolic order', in which the world of law and the social community is defined (turn back to the account of Lacan's theory in Section 3 if this idea isn't clear to you). But does her gender cause a girl to experience this process differently from a boy? Given the pervasively masculine nature of the symbolic order within patriarchal societies, it seems likely that the answer to this question will be yes. If so, how will this difference manifest itself? Feminism and psychoanalysis have combined to point to a continuing barrier between women and the most prestigious public modes of discourse. The novel, most often concerned with domestic rather than public affairs, had established itself as a partial exception to this rule, and its primary location within the home had made it the form easiest of access for women. Other modes of discourse remain problematic. And the implications of these cultural divisions extend far beyond literature. How many female philosophers can you name? Composers? Mathematicians? Theologians?

6.9 Lacan claims that the child must reject the maternal presence and accept the intervention of the father, representing the symbolic order, if it is to achieve a social identity. His argument suggests that if the social destiny of a girl is to become a mother, she must be identified with what all children must leave behind in order to acquire the status of a speaking adult. In taking on the culturally defined role of a woman, therefore, the adolescent girl can only claim the power of public speech at the expense of fracturing the internalized process that gives her a position within her culture. Such speech therefore becomes difficult for all women, impossible for many. You may remember Hélène Cixous's vivid evocation of what it feels like to be caught up in this predicament:

> Every woman knows the torment of getting up to speak. Her heart racing, at times entirely lost for words, ground and language slipping away – that's how daring a feat, how great a transgression it is for a woman to speak – even just open her mouth – in public. A double distress, for even if she transgresses, her words fall almost always upon the deaf male ear, which hears in language only that which speaks in the masculine.
>
> ('The laugh of the Medusa', Reader, p.321)

6.10 This line of thinking suggests why fragmentation, hysteria and madness have been inseparable from women's association with poetry, for if poetry is defined as one of the highest and most prestigious forms of public speech, it follows that women should find it particularly hard to claim access to it.

ACTIVITY

But male poets too may not find such access easy to claim. Here, for instance, is an early poem by T.S. Eliot. How do you think it relates to the issues we have been thinking about?

> **Hysteria**
>
> As she laughed I was aware of becoming involved in her laughter and being part of it, until her teeth were only accidental stars with a talent for squad-drill. I was drawn in by short gasps, inhaled at each momentary recovery, lost finally in the dark caverns of her throat, bruised by the ripple of unseen muscles. An elderly waiter with trembling hands was hurriedly spreading a pink and white checked cloth over the rusty green iron table, saying: 'If the lady and gentleman wish to take their tea in the garden, if the lady and gentleman wish to take their tea in the garden...' I decided that if the shaking of her breasts could be stopped, some of the fragments of the afternoon might be collected, and I concentrated my attention with careful subtlety to this end.

DISCUSSION

The title of the poem offers an important clue. In 1917, when T.S. Eliot wrote this poem, the word 'hysteria' had acquired a specialized meaning in psychoanalytic theory, as a neurotic condition in which repressed complexes became split off from the personality, causing a range of physical and emotional disorders. Women were identified as being particularly prone to hysteria: the word is in fact derived from the Greek *hystera*, meaning womb.

The form of the poem, too, has something to tell us, for it hardly manages to be a poem at all. It carries all the characteristics of prose, and could almost be an extract from a short story. A man and a woman are taking tea together; she has succumbed to a fit of uncontrollable laughter. Her companion feels alarmingly drawn in by her laughter, which threatens to swallow him. His afternoon is fragmented. Only if the woman can be stilled can he hope to reassemble it.

You might well have felt this to be a peculiarly exaggerated example of an alarmed male response to a woman opening her mouth in a public place. Particularly upsetting, perhaps, that she is laughing (did you recall Cixous's equally unruly laughing Medusa?), rather than uttering rational speech. And yet it is not quite clear whose the hysteria is, for isn't the man's response to the woman's merriment off-balance, disproportionately intense? There seems to be a strong element of sexual fear in the poem – the dread of being swallowed by a rapacious woman, overwhelmed by her 'hysteria'. The fear of neurotic women is a marked element of Eliot's early poetry, and is prominent in *The Waste Land*. Writing about such women is a way of controlling them, objectifying the disruption that they seem to represent. One element in the Modernist insistence on cool, hard, impersonal and unemotional poetry is the wish to dissociate the poetic from cultural constructions of femininity. James Joyce claimed that *The Waste Land* 'ended the idea of poetry for ladies' (Richard Ellman, quoted in Belsey and Moore, 1989, p.85).

ACTIVITY

I want finally to turn to the extract from Cora Kaplan's 'Language and gender' printed in the Reader (pp.310–16). Please read it now.

How does Kaplan build upon the psychoanalytical arguments that I have just summarized?

DISCUSSION

One of the most interesting developments in Kaplan's position, it seems to me, is that like many British feminists writing in the 1970s, she reads Lacan from a Marxist perspective. The gender-related issues surrounding poetry as 'a privileged metalanguage' have to do with the development of the child as an individual, but the inward pressures identified by psychoanalysis also give rise to social and political consequences of the widest kind. Kaplan asserts the need to 'acknowledge that control of high language is a crucial part of the power of dominant groups, and understand that the refusal of access to public language is one of the major forms of the oppression of women within a social class as well as in trans-class situations' (p.312). In other words, Kaplan pushes Lacanian theory into a cultural context much broader than we might have expected to find. In her argument, the relationship between social classes, or races, is not separate from the complex relationship between differing gender identities.

One consequence of this wider outlook is that she is interested, like Woolf and Gilbert and Gubar, in literary history. How has women's poetry developed? What have the constraints been – and the opportunities? Kaplan's account ranges from the seventeenth to the twentieth century. The Romantic period is of particular significance to her argument, for Romantic theories of poetic language have proved to be persistently influential. The Wordsworthian account of the poet as 'a man speaking to men' was not a calculated attempt to exclude women – such, however, has been its effect. Kaplan points out that the Romantic reverence for nature, too, has proved problematic for women poets. In practical terms, the wilder phenomena of nature were simply not as accessible to women as to their male counterparts. Long solitary walks over moor and mountain were hardly feasible for women – particularly for mothers of small children. In other ways, too, the identification of nature as the central matter of poetry has made the work of women poets still more complicated. For nature, given a symbolic status as 'Nature', is always defined as a feminine force to which the male poet pays his tribute of expressive homage. Here is yet another way in which the feminine is identified as the material of poetry rather than as the potential author. Kaplan ends her essay on an upbeat note. Long-standing cultural obstacles may be removed, even the deep difficulties which psychoanalysis reveals. Women *can* write poetry, more poetry and better poetry than they have ever written, once they identify and understand the barriers that have lain in their way. Did you find this optimism convincing? The poetry you will read in the following sections will help you to make up your mind.

7 Stevie Smith

7.1 If you'd never heard of Stevie Smith (1902–71) before embarking on this course, you might well have supposed her to be a man. Christened Florence Margaret Smith, Stevie was in fact known as 'Peggy' throughout her early years. She acquired her nickname while out riding in her late teens; her characteristically spirited style reminded a group of watching boys of the popular jockey Steve Donoghue, and the name they shouted after her stuck. The incident, and the name, are revealing. Stevie Smith was never quite content to remain within the boundaries of what was expected of a young lady of her generation. She did not marry, always earned her own living, and adopted an eccentrically unfeminine mode of dressing. And she became a poet.

7.2 Yet to think of her as a feisty feminist rebel would not be quite accurate. In many ways her life appeared sheltered and uneventful. Born in Hull in 1902, she moved with her mother, aunt and older sister to Palmer's Green, a peaceful London suburb, when she was three years old. She was to spend the rest of her life there. Her father abandoned the family, an event that left a permanent mark on Stevie Smith's mind. After the death of her mother, she lived with her much-loved aunt – the lion aunt, as she called her, 'a lion with a spanking tail who will have no nonsense' (*The Holiday*). For thirty years, she worked as a secretary to Sir Neville Pearson, in the publishing firm of Newnes. The job was undemanding, if unrewarding, and left time for writing. She made a name for herself with her first book, *Novel on Yellow Paper* (1936), which gave her an entry to the literary world. She led an active social life, and contact with other writers and critics was always important to her work. Stevie Smith wrote two further novels: *Over the Frontier* (1935) and *The Holiday* (1949). But her first commitment was to poetry, and it was as a poet that she became most widely known. She was astonishingly prolific, producing eight volumes in all and publishing regularly in periodicals. Her poems were usually accompanied by her own line drawings, which she always insisted were inseparable from their meaning. The drawings, she said, sometimes came first, suggesting the idea for a poem.

7.3 After her first success in the 1930s, her work went through a period of unpopularity, and it was not easy to get it published. Depression followed, and in 1953 she attempted suicide. But in the 1960s, her career unexpectedly prospered. Public poetry-readings gave scope to her talent for reading her poems aloud in her strangely distinctive voice, and gained her a new audience. In her final years she attained popular success as never before, and her achievements were formally recognized when she was awarded the Queen's Gold Medal for Poetry in 1969. She died in 1971.

AUDIO-CASSETTE

Recordings of Stevie Smith reading her own poems are included on Audio-cassette 4 Side 1, which accompanies this section. The purpose of this cassette is to help you to make an initial approach to the variety and subtlety of Stevie Smith's work, and to show how much is to be gained from listening to her poems rather than simply reading them. If you have not yet listened to this cassette, you will find it helpful to do so now.

A woman poet?

7.4 Did being a woman matter to Stevie Smith's work? There is a sense in which she wanted the answer to that question to be no. She distrusted the category of 'woman writer', feeling that what is best in a poet's work has nothing to do with gender. In her view, distinctions between masculine and feminine writing only emerge in the second-rate:

> Differences between men and women poets are best seen when the poets are bad. Bad women poets are better characters, they seldom … get drunk … go to prison … shoot the pianist. Their faults are soulfulness and banality. They like to commune (who does not?) with the Deity, Nature, themselves, but the words they use do not quite carry the traffic. Bad men poets are even more knowing; often they achieve fame as poets by stopping writing and going on committees.
>
> (*The Observer* 19 May 1968; quoted in Barbera and McBrien, 1981, p.181)

You will notice that Stevie Smith doesn't claim that there are no differences between men and women. Her half-serious account conforms to a familiar pattern: women are expected to lead inoffensive lives (as of course she did herself) and to write portentous but blandly conventional poetry. Men are more prone to shelter behind the kind of public status represented by committees. Her point is not that the categories of gender don't exist, but that the most worthwhile poetry transcends them.

7.5 This is a position with which you may well sympathize. It's one that many women poets (as opposed to feminist critics) have held, and unsurprisingly: if, as I've argued in the previous section, the position of women poets in our culture has by definition been subordinate, or at least problematic, then it has hardly been in the interests of women who want to be identified as significant poets to allow their sex to label their writing. Elizabeth Jennings puts this point of view in TV14, *Changing Voices.* To be called a 'woman poet' might seem to imply an unalterably second-class status in the literary world, with a restricted readership and confined range of subject matter. No wonder women have been reluctant to accept the term.

7.6 How far, then, can we accept the view that what matters most in Stevie Smith's writing is separate from gender?

ACTIVITY

Let's begin by looking at a short reflective poem in which she thinks about the motives of her writing. It's called 'My Muse', and you'll find it in the Poetry Anthology. Please read it now. What kind of poem is it? Does it seem to you to shed any light on the question of how being a woman might have shaped Stevie Smith's writing? And what do you make of that curious little drawing that goes with it?

DISCUSSION

The marked simplicity of 'My Muse' might be what struck you first. In his discussion of the poetry recorded on Audio-cassette 4 Side 1, John Purkis emphasizes how the complexity of Stevie Smith's poems is often concealed by an apparent artlessness. Would you agree that this is an example of such a poem? There are no obscurities of language. 'My Muse' is short, bare and direct, and it draws a melancholy conclusion. Only unhappiness, Stevie Smith tells us, enables her to exercise her poetic gifts. An unsophisticated poem, then – and a gloomy one?

Is this how you felt about it? How far does the accompanying drawing confirm such a view? That lank-haired and drooping Muse certainly doesn't look very cheerful. But isn't her exaggerated dejection comic? And isn't there something laughable about the poem as a whole? Look again at the final line – 'For my Muse this cannot but be dispiriting'. The dry formality of the language is deliberately deflating. Surely the position of the Muse is made to seem absurd rather than tragic?

How does the whole idea of having a Muse fit in with being a woman poet? The ancient tradition of the inspirational Muse who enabled a favoured poet to write is by no means genderless. If poets have most often been male, their Muses have always been female. From the first origins of Western culture, the Muse has been defined in the shape of a woman, conferring her divine gifts on chosen men: 'And he is lucky whom the Muses love', as the Greek poet Hesiod put it in the eighth century BC (*Theogony*, 1.98). Stevie Smith doesn't reject this convention – her lugubrious Muse is certainly female. But the traditional model of poetic creativity – the poet who loves and is loved by the Muse – is not available to her in any simple way. She can't easily choose to identify herself with the dignified voices of poetry's classical past – as poets from Milton to T.S. Eliot have so often done. There is a sense of exclusion in the poem: Stevie Smith's Muse is out 'in the cold'. When she is happy, at one with herself, she doesn't write.

Does 'My Muse' simply confirm a stereotyped picture of women's poetry? A picture of anguished unhappiness and cultural isolation? Not altogether, I'd say. The poem doesn't take itself quite seriously enough for that. It uses the tradition of the Muse, but it also sends it up. If it's a mourning voice that we hear, isn't it a mocking one too? Stevie Smith may be writing as an outsider here, but it's a situation that isn't wholly to her disadvantage.

Tradition and eccentricity

7.7 How far is Stevie Smith an outsider? She has certainly been seen as one. Critics writing about her poetry – and they have not been specially numerous, compared with those who have turned their attention to the poetry of (say) Eliot or Yeats – have tended to focus on the isolation of her work. She is often seen as a 'character', fashioning a uniquely individual voice out of the tranquillity of a secluded life. Seamus Heaney wrote of her in 1976, five years after her death: 'I suppose in the end the adjective has to be 'eccentric'. She looks at the world with a mental squint, there is a disconcerting wobble in the mirror she holds up to nature' (Heaney, 1980, p.201). Heaney is ambivalent about Stevie Smith's work. He admires her for the 'peculiar emotional weather between the words, a sense of pity for what is infringed and unfulfilled'. At the same time, he argues that her poems fail to attain 'the kind of large orchestration they are always tempting us to listen for' (pp.200–1). His mixed feelings seem to have more to do with his sense that she is confined by nationality and class rather than by gender. Heaney contends that Stevie Smith's characteristic voice is primarily that of the English middle class, arguing that 'it is essential to bring to the appreciation of these poems an ear aware of the *longueurs* and acerbities, the nuanced understatements and tactical intonations of educated middle-class English speech. The element this work survives in is disenchanted gentility...'

7.8 His objections make no reference to Smith's femininity. Nevertheless, the assumptions that underlie Heaney's judgement may be seen to bear some relationship to his sense of her gender. He writes: 'These odd syncopated melancholy poems are haunted by the primitive and compelling music of ballad and nursery rhyme, but it has been transposed by a sophisticated and slightly cosseted poetic ear into a still, sad, drawing-room music of humanity'. The 'primitive' forms of ballad and nursery rhyme have customarily been associated with women (you will recall Gilbert and Gubar's discussion of this point in the Reader extract, pp.27–33), but Heaney sees this conventionally feminine poetic identity as diminished by the genteel confinements of the drawing-room – another traditionally feminine territory – which have constrained her echoes of Wordsworth's 'still, sad music of humanity' (Heaney is quoting from Wordsworth's 'Lines Composed a Few Miles above Tintern Abbey'). The result, in Heaney's view, is a fundamental deficiency in her work: 'finally the voice, the style, the literary resources are not adequate to the sombre recognitions, the wounded *joie de vivre*, the marooned spirit we sense they were destined to express' (p.201). The implications of Heaney's charge are familiar. Writing as a woman, Stevie Smith seems to lack the kind of poetic resources that would have enabled her to treat major themes successfully.

7.9 Philip Larkin, in a generally sympathetic review (written in 1962) which had a good deal to do with the rehabilitation of Stevie Smith's reputation as a poet, was more forthright about what he feels to be the shortcomings of her writing as a woman. 'Her mode of writing, broadly speaking, is that of the *fausse-naïve*, the "feminine" doodler or jotter who puts down everything as it strikes her, no matter how silly or tragic, in a kind of Gertrude Stein-Daisy Ashford-Lorelei Lee way' (Larkin, 1983, p.153). Here is another familiar allegation: Stevie Smith's work is illogical – she can't think. But Larkin went on to praise Smith's writing for something that Heaney finds lacking – its scope. Larkin claimed that:

> the truth of the matter is that her talent is, as she translates Rimbaud's line, 'drawn by everything in turn'. Almost anything can strike her, and she will have a stab at conveying just how it made her feel – a singing cat, Cranmer, Copernicus, fourteen-year-old girls ... and thoughts and reflections that are hardly more than twists and grace-notes of the mind such as no one else would ever attempt to put into words.
>
> (pp.157–8)

Larkin and Heaney are in agreement about Stevie Smith's eccentricity, but Larkin sees a substance that outweighs it. 'For all the freaks and sports of her fancy ... Miss Smith's poems speak with the authority of sadness' (p.158).

7.10 It's hardly unusual to find critics in disagreement about a poet's work. And Heaney and Larkin are primarily poets rather than critics: in writing about Smith, they have something to say about themselves. Heaney's Irishness leads him to question the values of the English middle classes, while Larkin's work, as consciously English as that of Stevie Smith, consistently aspires to 'the authority of sadness'. But both Larkin and Heaney see their writing as part of a tradition, produced to express and defend a body of shared meaning. As Larkin put it, writing about the American poet Emily Dickinson in 1970, 'Poetry is an affair of sanity, of seeing things as they are. The less a writer's work approximates to this maxim, the less claim he has on the attention of his contemporaries and of posterity' (p.197). If we were to accept this as a criterion for poetic success (does it seem to you a workable one?), it's clear that supposedly 'eccentric' women poets like Stevie Smith (or, in Larkin's account, Emily Dickinson) will fall short. The 'mental squint' of a woman poet, her cultural oddity, will prevent her from 'seeing things as they are', excluding her from the approval of *her* (Larkin has 'his' – did you notice that assumption?) contemporaries and of posterity.

7.11 But if Stevie Smith – seen in this light – is an outsider, how far is any poet an insider? Like Heaney, Larkin supports his argument by appealing to a nineteenth-century ideal for poetry. Heaney, we've noticed, alludes to Wordsworth, while the origin of Larkin's phrase 'seeing things as they are' is the Victorian poet and critic Matthew Arnold, who saw dispassionate sanity as the highest cultural ideal. But Arnold believed that it was the critic, rather than the poet, who could best express such rational objectivity. He turned from poetry to prose, on the grounds that his own poems were too enervating and depressing to serve the needs of an age in search of spiritual sustenance. Nor is Wordsworth always sanguine about the poet's destiny: 'We poets in our youth begin in gladness /But thereof come in the end despondency and madness' ('Resolution and Independence', 1807). The Western cultural traditions which have associated poetry with exclusion, isolation, melancholy and madness are by no means confined to the poetry of women. It's worth thinking back, here, to your work on *écriture féminine* in Section 3. That 'disconcerting wobble' that Heaney points to, the 'feminine' doodling perceived by Larkin – can these be seen as evidence of a Kristevan semiotic at work in Smith's writing?

7.12 Stevie Smith was sharply aware of the cultural dilemmas inseparable from poetry. I want to turn now to her poem 'Thoughts about the Person from Porlock', published in 1962. Here she too alludes to the poetry of the nineteenth century. She is thinking about a celebrated poem by Wordsworth's friend Samuel Taylor Coleridge. Coleridge's 'Kubla Khan' (1816) records a wild dream of an enchanted 'pleasure-dome' – but it is unfinished. Coleridge attached a note to 'Kubla Khan', explaining that he was interrupted in the middle of writing it:

> At this moment he was unfortunately called out by a person on business from Porlock, and detained by him above an hour, and on his return to his room, found, to his no small surprise and mortification, that though he still retained some vague and dim recollection of the general purport of the vision, yet, with the exception of some eight or ten scattered lines or images, all the rest had passed away like the images on the surface of a stream into which a stone has been cast, but, alas! without the after restoration of the latter!

ACTIVITY

Please read 'Thoughts about the Person from Porlock' (Poetry Anthology) now. Does it have anything in common with 'My Muse'? How does it relate to the image of Stevie Smith as an eccentric outsider? Does the associated sketch have anything to add to the poem?

DISCUSSION

This is clearly a much longer and more ambitious poem than 'My Muse'. Nevertheless, a number of points of comparison might have struck you. It is, like 'My Muse', a literary poem, and it assumes that the reader has had something of a literary education – enough to recognize the allusion to the 'person from Porlock', at any rate. Does that make it obscure? Not really, I'd say. Despite its occasionally dry and formal vocabulary ('felicitate', 'benison'), the language is generally simple. And the theme? Like 'My Muse' ('For my muse, this cannot but be dispiriting'), 'Thoughts about the Person from Porlock' deals with sadness – in this case, with the longing for death ('These thoughts are depressing I know'). But I'd argue that it, too, can't really be said to be dismal. It doesn't seem to take itself wholly seriously ('There I go again') – like 'My Muse'. Would you agree that this is another poem that mocks as much as it mourns?

You might want to argue that it doesn't take literature quite seriously either. Coleridge, after all, is a poet of immense prestige, who certainly took himself very seriously indeed, and 'Kubla Khan' is one of his most revered works. He doesn't seem to cut a very imposing figure here – 'weeping and wailing: I am finished, finished'. If we take the puzzled and unhappy little figure accompanying the poem as a representation of Coleridge himself (it might, of course, depict the 'person from Porlock' – what do you think?), it would be hard to see anyone looking less like a distinguished poet and philosopher. He (or she? – would you agree that the sex of the figure is curiously indeterminate?) looks no more dignified, in fact, than that drooping Muse sitting beside the text of 'My Muse'.

Is such scepticism a reason to see Stevie Smith as an outsider? For all her evident Englishness, she perpetually derides the bodies of shared values, the ideologies, that bind English society together: Christianity (Stevie Smith's attack on the 'One Above' in this poem is characteristic), literary tradition, military conformity, family piety. She undermines English solemnities in all their forms. If this is a voice of gentility, it is also a voice that ridicules gentility ('his grandmother was a Warlock'). There seems to be no group with which Stevie Smith is prepared to identify.

7.13 Some degree of isolation might be seen as a characteristic of poets in general. In Stevie Smith's case, the implications have a great deal to do with her relationship with traditions of poetic language. Seamus Heaney, you will recall, felt that her work missed the 'large orchestration they are always tempting us to listen for'. What do you think he might have meant by that? How might such 'large orchestration' have worked?

7.14 I think that what Heaney has in mind here is very much a matter of language. Stevie Smith's subversion of the grander resonances of poetry, its claim to create a world of transcendent meaning, is not in itself an exceptional feature of the poetry of her period, and it's an impulse clearly not confined to women poets. You will be able to think of others (Auden is an example that comes to mind) who were attempting something similar. But few other poets were so thoroughgoing in their insistence on the oddness of perception, and the frequent absurdity of attempts to communicate even the most momentous experiences. Few were prepared to hazard making their work ridiculous – a serious risk for a poet after all, and one that Stevie Smith has always been ready to take.

ACTIVITY

As an example let's look at 'The Jungle Husband' – a poem that Stevie Smith often included in her public performances (a recording of her reading the poem is included on Audio-cassette 4 Side 1; you will find the text in the Poetry Anthology). Please read it now. What happens in this poem?

DISCUSSION

Confronted with the immensities of primitive nature, Wilfred dutifully attempts to convey his adventures to his wife Evelyn. Would you agree that he fails so completely that the result is irresistibly comic ('It is all gray /But green on top…')? But the poem has, I think, a serious point. Wilfred – his name gives him away – can't manage a convincing masculine heroism, despite his hunting exploits and solitary expeditions into the wild ('Tomorrow I am going alone a long way /Into the jungle…'). Compare him for a moment with Hemingway's Wilson. Would Wilson's manly reticence have been quite so impressive if he'd been called Wilfred?

Here it's worth remembering the power of laughter, a weapon shared by subversive women of many differing persuasions – from Kate Millett's stinging derision of Lawrence to Cixous's laughing Medusa. The absurdity of Stevie Smith's language in 'The Jungle Husband' is an attack on a further species of dignified rhetoric – this time, on the masculine rhetoric of the hunter nobly triumphing over an untamed and perilous nature. In the words of the French philosopher Annie Leclerc, 'One must simply deflate his values with the needle of ridicule' (in Marks and de Courtivron, 1981, p.79; see also Sections 1 and 3).

7.15 Stevie Smith didn't see this particular rhetoric as being confined to escapades in the jungle stew. The language of the masterful male is one of her commonest targets, in her fiction as well as her poetry.

ACTIVITY

A short extract from her novel *Over the Frontier* is included in the Prose Anthology (pp.128–30). Please read it now. How does it compare with 'The Jungle Husband'?

DISCUSSION

For the first few paragraphs at least, you might have felt this extract to be a treatment of very much the same subject. Tom's bossy behaviour reminds Pompey of the jungle husbands of Bottle Green (her fictional name for Palmer's Green), who, like Wilfred, swagger and issue orders in a ludicrous way. But it soon becomes clear that, here, Stevie Smith is writing about something more than the absurdity of masculine pretension. After all, the commanding Tom is compared with a female figure of authority ('This very explicit Nanny-Tom...'). It is her riding clothes that Pompey finds laid out for her; riding, for Stevie Smith, is always an image of assertion and control (it was her brisk style of riding, remember, that first earned her nickname). Pompey is horrified to discover that the 'tight hard sentry box of a coat' she is to wear, is that of a masculine military uniform, representing the savagery she most abhors. Women are not, it appears, immune from the dangers of conformism: and Stevie Smith was always aware that she was as liable to fall into its poisoned snares as anyone else.

7.16 *Over the Frontier* was published in 1938, a year when the image of suddenly finding yourself in an unwanted uniform was particularly topical. Stevie Smith had visited Germany twice, in 1929 and 1931; she had seen something of the rise of Nazism, and came to feel that war was inevitable. In 1938, she wrote despairingly in the *London Mercury*: 'Is the human race then never to be trusted round the corner where the hobby-horses of ideology neigh?' (quoted in Spalding, 1989, p.136). Stevie Smith was never a political writer in the sense that Auden (for a while) was: 'I am not interested to concentrate upon politics, fascism or communism, or upon any groupismus whatever' (*Over the Frontier*, p.256). Nevertheless, there is a sense in which politics were a motive for her writing. Politics, like religion (compare those sinister infant devotees in 'Our Bog is Dood', discussed in the audio-cassette recording), might become a means to muffle our perceptions, to wrap ourselves up with a self-importance that makes us cruel. Stevie Smith cherished no gentle fantasies about human nature. *Over the Frontier* reaches a remarkably unfeminine conclusion: 'power and cruelty are the strength of our life, and in its weakness only is there the sweetness of love.'

7.17 Stevie Smith is not a comfortable poet. All the great remedies which humanity has proposed to dignify or palliate its suffering (religion, patriotism, politics, love) are questioned and found wanting in her poems, and she returns to the wish for death again and again. But even unhappiness can seem absurd. 'Scorpion' expresses a central contradiction in her work: you'll find the poem in the Poetry Anthology. Stevie Smith wrote it towards the end of her life, at a time of acute depression: 'It is just what I feel like. Except one feels so much better for having said it.' Yet 'Scorpion' is hardly a tragic poem. The suicidal scorpion is pitiable, but isn't she (or he?) too cantankerous to be tragic? 'Other souls can find somewhere *else*.' The self-absorbtion of Scorpion's misery is laughable – though its predicament is not. If you find the poem funny (opinions about whether a poem is funny or not will always vary), would you agree that it is (in Stevie Smith's words) 'not a humour one would care to meet on a dark night' (Barbera and McBrien, 1985, p.244)?

7.18 I want to end by leaving you with some questions about Stevie Smith's distinctive language. The title of this block is 'Language and Gender', and you've already given a good deal of thought to the complex relationships between language and our culturally constructed concepts of masculinity and femininity. How far do you think the extraordinary irreverence we've found in Stevie Smith's writing, its persistent tendency to mock the most powerful cultural institutions, is a product of her writing as a woman? What about its capacity to move rapidly between different and sometimes contradictory themes and moods? Are these features of her work that might lead you to claim her as an example of *écriture féminine*? Think, too, about the way in which she has been read – by other poets, thinking about their own work; by me, writing for this course; by you, as a student. If Stevie Smith had been a man, would her work have found a different reception? And would that have been to her advantage?

8 *Sylvia Plath*

The disquieting muse

8.1 Sylvia Plath was born on 27 October 1932 in Boston, Massachusetts, of German–Austrian parentage. Her early years in the seashore town of Winthrop, Massachusetts, were remembered as idyllic. But on 2 November 1940 her father died, after a long and difficult illness. Apparently she worshipped him, and his death features as a central, disturbing element in her writing. The family moved inland, to the upper-middle-class Boston suburb of Wellesley, where Mrs Plath went to work as a teacher, and Sylvia's grandmother assumed the care of the household. Whereupon those first years 'sealed themselves off like a ship in a bottle – beautiful, inaccessible, obsolete, a fine, white, flying myth' ('OCEAN 1212–W', quoted in Newman, 1970, p.272).

8.2 At the same time Plath's writing began, and it was poetry from the start. The family used to read aloud. On one occasion her mother read out Matthew Arnold's 'The Forsaken Merman' and, as her daughter later recalled, 'A spark flew off Arnold and shook me, like a chill. I wanted to cry; I felt very odd. I had fallen into a new way of being happy' ('OCEAN 1212–W', op. cit., p.267).

Although she went on to write short stories and a novel, Sylvia Plath's main interest remained poetry, which she continued to work at with great deliberation throughout a brilliant academic career, culminating with her return in 1957 to the expensive and exclusive Smith College (Massachusetts), which she had first attended on a scholarship. Now she was a teacher of 'freshman' (first-year) English, a published writer, and married to the poet Ted Hughes, whom she had met while on a Fulbright Scholarship at Cambridge University. Working together in an intensely productive and creative relationship, although writing 'poems that are as distinct and different as our fingerprints must be' (quoted in Aird, 1973, p.10), she and Hughes soon decided to devote all their energies to their writing, living on their savings and small jobs.

8.3 Early in 1960 Plath and Hughes moved to London, where their first child was born. Almost simultaneously, Plath's first book of poems, and the only one to appear in her lifetime, *The Colossus*, was accepted for publication; and Ted Hughes's second collection, *Lupercal*, appeared. By the summer of 1961 she and Hughes had left London for an old manor house in Devon, where she completed her novel *The Bell Jar*. She continued to write, while running the household with the efficiency that was evident in everything she did. In January 1962 her son was born. The poetry arising from her experience as a mother has been widely influential and of great interest to women poets – Carol Rumens cites her example in TV14. The birth marked a period of extraordinary creative achievement which was cut short tragically a year later when she took her own life, having returned with her children to London to live apart from Hughes. She was thirty.

8.4 Since Sylvia Plath's suicide and the posthumous publication of *The Bell Jar* (1963) and *Ariel* (1965), her name has become known well beyond the usual literary circles. Inevitably, the sudden end to her life and her relationship with a major English poet, aroused much morbid curiosity, and still does. As I write, yet another biography has been published (by the poet Anne Stevenson), attended by yet more speculation and controversy about the details of her life, relationships and – especially – her death. The writer and critic Al Alvarez (b.1929), poetry editor of *The Observer* and her first champion, tried to provide a relatively impersonal account of her last months of fierce creativity in his book on suicide, *The Savage God* (1971), in which he told of a lonely but determined woman who took her life almost accidentally, as the last of a series of gambles with death – the first of these, ten years before, was an attempted suicide as a student at Smith. But Alvarez also encouraged the myth-making by appearing to argue that mental instability was necessary, if not suicidal tendencies, for the kind of poetry she produced: 'Poetry of this order is a murderous art', he concluded (Alvarez, 1963, p.26).

8.5 Alvarez was promoting a particular kind of modern poetry, poetry committed to an exploration of the hidden roots of fear, guilt and anxiety within the individual which, he claimed, also reflected the darkly hostile forces at work in history. For him, and those who shared his views, American poets such as Plath and Robert Lowell (and English poets such as Hughes) were in this way bringing new life to the English poetic tradition in the late fifties and early sixties. More important for the development of the Plath legend, however, was the fact that she quickly became a representative female victim of the patriarchal world: according to the American feminist poet Robin Morgan, Sylvia Plath was the victim of a 'conspiracy' to

> mourn [her] brilliance while
> patronizing her madness, diluting her rage,
> burying her politics.
>
> (Morgan, 'Arraignment', 1972)

In this sense, she is both an obvious choice for study here, and a very tricky one, since her writings come laden with preconceptions about their relevance and value.

8.6 Where, then, should we start? There's no doubt about the brilliantly disturbing and subversive force of her work, nor of the rage and the sense of persecution it conveys. But rage towards whom, exactly? Or, persecution by what? In one of her best-known poems, 'Lady Lazarus', she concluded:

> Out of the ash
> I rise with my red hair
> And I eat men like air.
>
> (1965, p.19)

Quoted out of context, or simply related to her equally famous poem 'Daddy', with its equally well-known concluding words: 'Daddy, daddy, you bastard, I'm through', the answers may appear self-evident. Men are the enemy, to be angrily dismissed or destroyed.

8.7 But what about, say, her poem 'The Disquieting Muses', in which the threat originates from the mother – and, indeed, female powers in general? That poem commemorates the rejection of the mother's well-meaning attempts to turn the daughter into an image of middle-class achievement, offering gingerbread and piano lessons; and it goes on to propose the alternative of the female 'Muses' of the title. However, these alternative 'muses' are blank-faced and stony, 'Their shadows long in the setting sun /That never brightens or goes down' (1960, p.59). In short, even more threatening in their way. And a few days after composing 'Daddy', she wrote 'Medusa' (*Ariel*, pp.45–6), in which it is, again, the mother whose deadly effect upon her daughter is proposed: she is both the classical-mythological figure whose gaze turns those who meet it to stone, and the sea-nettle whose 'umbilicus' paralyses those it touches. In so far as 'nature' is Plath's subject too, it is ambivalent, liberating as well as threatening – as you may recall from Block 1 and the discussion there of 'Blackberrying', in which the 'blood sisterhood' that the narrator feels imposed upon her is also strangely welcome.

8.8 In short, the Plath legend has obscured the range an ' complexity of her work, and the feelings expressed in it. Not only are the anger and negation more complex than is commonly supposed, but, as we shall see, her work articulates more positive, integrating feelings, too. What we need to ask is *how* – in her carefully crafted and highly disciplined poems – do these feelings present themselves? And how does gender come into it?

Father-figures

8.9 Let's begin with the title-poem of *The Colossus*, the only collection of Sylvia Plath's poetry published in her lifetime. 'The Colossus' helps to introduce the dominant themes of her work and to show how they are worked out in detail. The colossus that provides the poem's basic metaphorical scheme is derived from the Colossus of Rhodes, a giant statue of the sun-god Apollo which was one of the seven wonders of the ancient world and which, according to popular tradition, bestrode the entrance of the harbour with ships passing between its legs. The actual statue (which was only 102 feet high and probably not even erected at the harbour) was demolished by an earthquake – hence the scattered pile of ruins over which the narrator of the poem is found clambering, hopelessly trying to reassemble it.

ACTIVITY

Now read the poem, and ask yourself: what is its subject? Is it purely personal? Or does it take on more general issues? You might like to check for yourself in a reference work the allusion, in the fourth stanza, to the *Oresteia* (by the Greek dramatist Aeschylus), since it provides an important clue to the poem's meaning. But you might also consider the imagery of speech and language in the poem: does it relate the personal to the general? And does it have to do with the issue of gender?

SAMPLE ANSWER/DISCUSSION

That cry in the fourth stanza, 'O father', immediately suggests that the helpless, absorbed figure crawling, ant-like and industrious, over the mammoth ruins of her god is a child searching for her dead father among the ruins of the distant past. She is also trying to find an identity – an identity which is perceived as recoverable from the gigantic 'other' which lies catastrophically dead and fragmented. There is an obvious sense in which identity comes from the father; equally, this is shown to be an insecure, perhaps impossible source. Hence the feeling of frustration and despair in the last lines. To read Sylvia Plath's poems is to come to the realization of their specific, personal – and thus gendered – cast again and again: details such as 'Thirty years now' relate to what we know about her as the author: her father in fact died only nineteen years before she wrote this; but she was thirty when it appeared.

So is the poem about a life spent fruitlessly trying to put together the image of her father? Surely – yes. We know this not only because of the biographical emphasis but also because of what the wrecked giant represents. This is where the more general level of meaning emerges. The massive ruin represents the institutions of a patriarchal society, and most notably those which have to do with *language*. Apollo is, of course, male; and he represents poetry and music as well as power. At first, the broken statue's 'speech' seems comic, even absurd, with those 'bawdy cackles' proceeding from its great lips. But in the second stanza comes the suggestion that it was 'an oracle', mouthpiece of 'the dead, or of some god or other'.

In its futile attempts to mend this god, literally to clear its throat, the child-woman is struggling to get access to the great, classical past of European tradition, at the same time as she struggles to discover what her dead father still has to say. Father, speech and cultural tradition coalesce into one massive, overwhelming, yet fractured image. The writing, the existence of the poem itself, implies the female articulacy that the conclusion appears to deny: thereby resisting that weighty taboo which, as Cora Kaplan points out (Reader, p.315), has silenced women for so long. When Sylvia Plath was at Cambridge, young women would come up to her and say, 'How do you dare to write, how do you dare to publish a poem, because of the criticism, the terrible criticism, that falls upon one if one does publish?'. That was when 'I first felt the full weight of English Literature' (Orr, 1966, pp.168–9).

Perhaps the narrator and the tiny *alter ego* don't have to be perceived as female; but if they're not, a whole dimension of the poem is lost. Perhaps we all in some sense crawl like ants in mourning over the remembered or dreamt-of, collapsed images of our parents; perhaps, too, in a Freudian reading, we all share the resentful, even aggressive emotions that underlie the poem, and are reinforced by that allusion to the *Oresteia* in stanza four. Aeschylus' series of plays is about the bloody family feuds of Agamemnon and Clytemnestra, and their offspring Orestes and Electra. The allusion is all the more forceful for being indirect, distancing the personal anguish which is allowed full play elsewhere in Plath – most notably in, for example, 'Electra on Azalea Path' (unpublished until after her death), in which she concluded:

> O pardon the one who knocks for pardon at
> Your gate, father – your hound-bitch, daughter, friend.
> It was my love that did us both to death.
>
> (in Hughes, 1981, p.117)

This is more personal and explicit: Azalea Path is where Otto Plath's grave lies. Electra survived to mourn the killing of her father Agamemnon by her mother Clytemnestra, and the death of the latter at the vengeful hands of Orestes, her brother. Guilt is the strongest emotion in 'Electra on Azalea Path', whereas loss is the strongest feeling conveyed by 'The Colossus'. 'The Colossus' appears to confirm Lacan's notion of the position of the childish self in its tragic search for meaning, developing language as part of, and in response to, a generalized sense of lack and fragmentation in its world (see paragraph 3.10). Nevertheless, reading it in terms of the development of the ungendered self seems to me to diminish its impact.

Sylvia Plath was all too aware of the childish guilt which produced her intensely ambivalent feelings towards her father. She is reported to have said: 'He was an autocrat. I adored and despised him, and I probably wished many times that he were dead. When he obliged me and died, I imagined that I had killed him' (quoted in Steiner, 1974, p.21). These (not uncommon) feelings undoubtedly lie beneath 'Daddy', one of her best-known and most sensationally intense poems. But there is more to it than that.

ACTIVITY

Please now read 'Daddy', in the Poetry Anthology. Then read Sylvia Plath's own explanatory note below, made for the BBC broadcast of 'Daddy'. What does it tell us about the poem? Think of what's just been said about the effect of 'The Colossus', and compare 'Daddy'. Does the Electra reference make sense? What do you make of the poem's subject and its manner, its language? Is 'Daddy' a political poem?

> Here is a poem spoken by a girl with an Electra complex. Her father died while she thought he was God. Her case is complicated by the fact that her father was also a Nazi and her mother very possibly part-Jewish. In the daughter the two strains marry and paralyse each other – she has to act out the awful little allegory once over before she is free of it.
>
> (quoted in Alvarez, 1963, pp.25–6)

SAMPLE ANSWER AND DISCUSSION

The detached, deliberate, generalizing tone of 'The Colossus' has disappeared, and what we have instead is, apparently, an 'awful little allegory' acted out or dramatized by the speaker in order to exorcize the 'Electra complex' from which she suffers – and it is unquestionably 'she', isn't it? The element of mournful nostalgia, of regret, in 'The Colossus' has become resentment, anger, even murderous resolve. The colloquial tone and the insistent, nursery rhyme pattern (echoing the same sound over and over) establish a bizarre, surrealistic but hypnotic effect that is hard to resist. But what is it saying?

The implication of 'Electra complex' appears to be that the narrator suffers from a condition analogous to the Oedipus complex: instead of the male child desiring his mother and experiencing his father as a threat he wishes to overcome by violence, the female child desires her father and experiences the mother as threatening. This analogy was proposed not by Freud (who in fact dismissed it) but by his follower, the Swiss Carl Gustav Jung, who developed it as part of his theory of an eternal feminine principle, which was then taken up by certain feminists, including de Beauvoir. Plath's version is 'complicated' by the paralysing effect of the historical interpretation she adds: her father 'a Nazi' and her mother 'very possibly part-Jewish'.

Needless to say, there is no biographical basis for these assumptions. This is a fantasy; yet, at the same time, it is grounded in the real familial feelings acknowledged by the poet in her various utterances, poetic, narrative and personal, as the allusions – to her teacher father's origins in the Polish town, to her suicide attempt at twenty – emphasize. The basic metaphor, of her father as a Nazi, is extended to include that subsequent father-figure, her husband (he to whom she says 'I do, I do'); both are incorporated by a remorseless, fairy-tale logic into a multitude of evil, folklore images, the black man who bites 'my pretty red heart in two', the vampire who gets staked to the ground to destroy his power; while the child-victim, metaphorically a Jew in the concentration camps, becomes a puppet to be glued together. The father's unreachable massiveness and god-like demeanour are more obviously gendered ('Marble-heavy, a bag full of God'); the inaccessibility of his language is now less a matter of its classical distance than its 'obscene' strangeness. The child's submissiveness becomes a horrifying, sado-masochistic image of cruelty welcomed, even adored.

It has been argued that this is a tender poem, even a love poem; and also that it is a poem of abuse, even hatred. Surely it is both? More important, what to make of the association of these intense, and intensely private feelings, with the public images of a known modern history? It's been argued that the manipulation of imagery from the Nazi era here (and in 'Lady Lazarus') is fraudulent, a way of merely pretending to a more than private meaning. My own view (which has differed at different times) is that 'Daddy' is more than personal in effect, not only because of how it expresses, as a kind of primitive truth, the connection between extremes of love and hate, affection and brutality, but also because of what has emerged about the connection between the formation of the masculine identity and fascism (for example in Klaus Theweleit's *Male Fantasies*, 1987, about the proto-Nazi *Freikorps*; see also what Ciceley Havely writes about Francis Macomber, paragraph 5.16). You will need to make up your own mind. In any case we will be coming back to the issue of poetry and history in Block 8.

Making and unmaking

8.10 Sylvia Plath observed of the poetry she was writing as she entered her last phase, the poetry of *Ariel*:

> My poems do not turn out to be about Hiroshima, but about a child forming itself finger by finger in the dark. They are not about the terrors of mass extinction, but about the bleakness of the moon over a yew tree in a neighbouring graveyard ... For me, the real issues of our time are the issues of every time – the hurt and wonder of loving; making in all its forms – children, loaves of bread, paintings, buildings; and the conservation of life of all people in all places...
>
> (quoted in Newman, 1970, p.33)

This enforces a recognition of the crucial difference between the different personae, the different experiences, conjured up in her last, astonishing burst of creativity. The poem which she placed at the beginning of *Ariel*, the collection including 'Daddy' and 'Lady Lazarus', was an *aubade*, traditionally addressed by a man to his lover, but here welcoming the arrival of her son. It is a beginning celebrating beginnings: 'Love set you going like a fat gold watch' was the opening line of 'Morning Song'. Birth, and rebirth, became recurrent images, to hold against the imagery of death and decay which she was exploring at the same time. Striving for perfection as she had all her life, she had also come to realize that 'Perfection is terrible, it cannot have children' ('The Munich Mannequins', *Ariel*, p.74). So she drew on the immediate experiences of her life as a mother increasingly isolated in a domestic setting – even describing a minor kitchen accident with her now customary dramatic aplomb: 'What a thrill – /My thumb instead of an onion' ('Cut'). The slow deliberation with which her earlier work grew was displaced by a revelatory intensity, a radically 'free' manner.

8.11 This isn't to suggest an absolute break between her earlier poetry and the later work – an interpretation readily produced by the Plath myth-makers, who always emphasize her last months. A helpful corrective is provided by 'Blackberrying', written after *The Colossus* poems, but before *Ariel*. Re-reading 'Blackberrying' now, you can tell how much it shares with her earlier and later work: the logical, progressive, rhetorical structure of *The Colossus*, as it moves towards the climactic image of the sea; and at the same time, the more arbitrary, associative and sinister imagery of 'Daddy', as it diverges towards that threatening hook, that violent din. Here, the evident gender dimension is important: those overripe berries evoking menstrual flow, a 'blood sisterhood', tying women together in the face of an overwhelming sense of meaninglessness, looking out 'on nothing, nothing but a great space'. How far is this a gendered vision? Or perhaps more important, how far does the gendered aspect of the poem produce a distinctively gendered discourse, an *écriture féminine*? We need to look at another poem, this time from *Ariel*, to find the terms for an answer.

ACTIVITY

Now please read 'Nick and the Candlestick', one of the 'domestic' poems occasioned by the birth of her son. How does the personal and autobiographical get transformed? How would you describe the language of the poem? Is it *écriture féminine*?

SAMPLE ANSWER AND DISCUSSION

The personal is finely generalized by means of the daring development of religious metaphor: love, faith and praise turning this particular baby into 'the baby in the barn', the Christ-child. The poem is colloquial, surprising and at first disjointed, jerkily presenting one bizarre association after another, then gradually settling down into an accepting, affirmative mode. The eighth stanza contains the turning-point (you may have to re-read the poem to appreciate this): 'O love, how did you get here?' Where is 'here'? The room in which the mother has imagined herself, like a miner in a cave, a space in which the everyday, homely objects of night-light and fish bowl seem cold, hostile, deadly; but the baby sleeps on, oblivious, its 'crossed position' an echo of its embryonic state, and a hopeful anticipation – through the religious overtones – of life continuing. Horror turns to joy, as white turns to red, in the colour symbolism of the poem. The possibility of death is never finally excluded: not only because of the physical reality of continuing cold, imagined as drips of mercury falling into the 'terrible well' of (atomic?) death; but also, of course, because of what we know about the Christ-child's future.

The logic of the poem's structure of associations seems both inward and arbitrary, witty and extreme, suggestive of the 'semiotic' discourse proposed by Kristeva. Even more striking, and by now familiar from the earlier poems we've looked at, is the irresolvably *contradictory* quality of this writing: the same image charged with violently opposed associations which do not really settle down into the 'unifying' experience we tend to expect even of modern poetry. As in a phrase such as 'piranha religion', what we have is a proliferation of metaphor which begins with unexpected resonances of opposing meanings, but which remains unsettled in resonance. Whether you call this *écriture féminine* or not will depend upon how far you consider it beyond the realm of masculine discourse. In any case, it seems to me that it has to do with a gender identity that is itself finally provisional, because it is both dependent upon, and always resisting, the patriarchal hierarchy of meaning.

One final example may clarify the issue. Certainly it suggests how central the problem of identity was to this poet – and, arguably, to the kind of writing she chose.

ACTIVITY

Please now read 'Mirror', which was written after 'The Colossus', but before the *Ariel* poems, and published posthumously. As Dinah Birch pointed out in Section 3, gazing into a mirror suggests a passivity and self-absorption traditionally presumed feminine; it is also an image for self-definition through others – through, if you like, the determining (patriarchal) 'Other'. How does Plath imagine the construction/destruction of the female identity here?

SAMPLE ANSWERS AND DISCUSSION

In a brilliant and striking reversal, we have the voice of the mirror itself speaking its awful truth about the woman who looks into it for her identity. At first witty and amusing, finally threatening and uncanny, the poem mines folkloric and classical sources for their unexpected resonances – I expect the idea of the poem derives, consciously or not, from that well-known childhood fairy story, in which the mirror tells the stepmother-queen what she does not want to hear, when she asks it: 'Mirror, mirror, on the wall, /Who's the fairest of them all?' The poem suggests women have to fear the answer to their anxious queries, as the 'young girl' in them is 'drowned' by time, and the 'old woman' rises 'day after day, like a terrible fish'.

Thus, the construction of a feminine identity is imagined as *simultaneously* destructive. Typically for Plath, there is a mythic resonance: the mirror is also a lake – the lake, no doubt, into which Narcissus peered, and where he fell in love with the reflection of himself, and so pined away. But a more frightening end is hinted at for the female gazer: to be drowned and eaten by her *alter ego*. The self-destructive implication (and we cannot easily forget Plath's own attempts) is apt, since the feminine gender is created by ingesting the cultural conditioning that proposes this construction of identity as an objective truth ('I am not cruel, only truthful').

Plath was not the first woman poet to try to formulate this: there is a remarkable poem by Christina Rossetti entitled 'Passing and Glassing', which struggles to find religious consolation through that 'wisdom' which arises as a result of contemplating the passing of all things in 'woman's looking-glass'. Nor is the subject exclusively a woman's topic: Thomas Hardy's 'I Look Into My Glass', mordantly reflecting upon his 'wasting skin' but 'throbbing' heart, suggests as much. And yet Hardy wrote a much more powerful meditation upon the subject when he adopted a female persona, in 'The Beauty', which dramatizes the alienating, self-destructive effect of masculine pressures upon a young and attractive woman. Reading Sylvia Plath's poems in terms of language and gender issues offers a way of re-reading poems by many others as well.

9 Elizabeth Bishop

9.1 Elizabeth Bishop was born in Massachusetts in 1911. After an unsettled childhood she went to Vassar College, a prestigious academy for women, where she graduated in 1934. During the late 1930s she travelled widely in Europe and North Africa. In 1946 her first collection of poems, *North and South*, was published to much critical acclaim. In 1951 she first visited Brazil where she decided to live for the next seventeen years. Her second book, *Poems*, which included a new collection entitled *A Cold Spring*, won the Pulitzer Prize in 1955. Two further collections of poetry were published: *Questions of Travel* (1965) and *Geography III* (1976). Towards the end of her life she divided her time between her home in Brazil and teaching at Harvard. She died in Boston in 1979.

9.2 Thus described, her education and career place her squarely in the mainstream of twentieth-century American poetry, a tradition dominated by largely male, frequently academic, poets. Her highbrow readership is indicated by the fact that the texts you will be reading here, as well as many others by her, were first published in the established American journals, *New Yorker* and *Partisan Review*. She was praised by the poet Robert Lowell for 'her bare objective language' (1947, p.498), and the critic Randall Jarrell saw 'in her best work restraint, calm and proportion ... implicit in every detail of organisation and workmanship' (1973, p.210). She has been celebrated recently by Seamus Heaney as 'this most reticent and mannerly of poets' (1988, p.101). Altogether her poetry represents one kind of gendered stereotype of the woman poet, that of formal restraint and propriety in language (completely at odds, though, with another pervasive gendered 'type', that of the uncontrollable muse, with which Plath is often associated). Like Stevie Smith, she distanced herself from the feminism of the sixties and after, and, so far, she has attracted little feminist literary criticism. She does not, it appears, fit tidily into the theme of this block: language and gender.

9.3 Yet two aspects of her life resist the comfortable appraisal sketched above and challenge the reader to examine more closely the role of language and gender in her work. First, the titles of her collections of poems, and her residence in Brazil for much of her adult life, register her preoccupation with geography, travel and place. That she lived much of her life in a kind of exile from her native culture and language is an issue the importance of which should be clear from your study of authors such as Walcott in Block 6. Secondly, her most intimate personal and literary friendships were with women. By her own account it was the poet Marianne Moore, over twenty years her senior, who was the most powerful single influence in shaping her career. Both factors emphasize that her characteristic detachment is more than simply a willingness to play the role of a retiring feminine intelligence.

9.4 In this section, you will be examining three poems and a short story by Elizabeth Bishop. As a way of focusing on the issues of this block – language and gender – these texts will be considered in the following subsections: 'Nature', 'Bishop's sense of historical knowledge', 'Gender and identity' and 'Women and madness'.

Nature

ACTIVITY

Please now read 'The Fish', which you will find in the Poetry Anthology.

(a) How would you describe the language and form of the poem?

(b) How is 'nature' perceived in 'The Fish'? In thinking about this question, you may like to compare 'The Fish' with Hughes' 'Pike', which is also in the anthology (and was discussed in Block 5).

DISCUSSION

(a) You may feel that the most obvious thing about the language of the poem is that it is descriptive. This is so especially for the first half of the poem down to: 'It was more like the tipping /of an object toward the light.' Conventionally, 'description' is associated with a neutral passivity on the part of the observer, in which the object is isolated from the subject examining it. But the point about 'The Fish' is surely that such detachment is shown to be impossible.

The way that the language resists being categorized as merely descriptive becomes explicit at the point when the speaker sees, 'five big hooks / grown firmly in his mouth'; after this, the emotional attitude of the speaker towards the fish becomes the focus of attention. But even within the apparently neutral observation of the first half of the poem, the possibility of an objective stance has already been undermined. The adjectives, 'battered and venerable /and homely' in the opening lines of the poem suggest the vulnerability, heroism and domesticity of the fish, with which the speaker later explicitly identifies.

One example of how the speaker's sensitivity is revealed can be found between the lines 'While his gills were breathing in' and 'like a big peony'. Notice how 'the frightening gills' are also vulnerable, 'fresh and crisp with blood, /that can cut so badly'; how what is aesthetically ugly, 'the coarse white flesh', is also delicate and fragile, 'packed in like feathers'. There are many other examples of this conjunction of opposites in the poem through which the speaker's compassion is revealed. Look closely at how the fish's skin and eyes are described.

In terms of form, 'The Fish' seems to be an example of poetry as straightforward narrative, a mode that, as you learned earlier in the course, Modernist techniques often disrupted. Bishop is explicit about the ostensible simplicity of much of her work. In an interview with Alexandra Johnson in the *Christian Science Monitor* in 1978, she said:

> The greatest challenge, for me, is to try to express difficult thoughts in plain language. I prize clarity and simplicity. I like to present complicated or mysterious ideas in the simplest possible way. This is a discipline which many poets don't see as important as I do.
>
> (Travisano, 1988, pp.63–4)

But while the poem eschews the Modernist enthusiasm for foregrounding literary technique, it does not employ an entirely impersonal language, especially in those final lines: 'until everything /was rainbow, rainbow, rainbow!' This is not simply a personal celebration, an epiphany of sorts, but can be understood as a defiant affirmation.

(b) I want to suggest that even in this apparently simple poem, there is a sense in which Bishop resists conventional views of 'nature'. The poem begins as a celebration of catching 'a tremendous fish' but ends as an even greater celebration of its release. Not only does the speaker come to identify sympathetically with the fish as a victim, but, more importantly perhaps, the poem ends by affirming that the utterly commonplace detail of the inside of the boat can be invested with beauty:

> I stared and stared
> and victory filled up
> the little rented boat,

from the pool of bilge
where oil had spread a rainbow
around the rusted engine
to the bailer rusted orange,
the sun-cracked thwarts,
the oarlocks on their strings,
the gunnels – until everything
was rainbow, rainbow, rainbow!
And I let the fish go.

This moment of liberated insight is as much a result of a transformed perception in the speaker as it is a consequence of the play of light, i.e. of 'nature'.

'Pike' is a very different kind of poem. Hughes sets up a dramatic contrast between the human observer and the alien, underwater world of the fish which symbolizes nature as a repressed and latently violent, unconscious force. In 'The Fish', Bishop avoids both anthropomorphism and symbolism (since neither human nor abstract qualities are invested in the fish), and she also avoids the violent struggle between the human and natural world implicit in 'Pike'. Reading Hughes's poem as masculine and Bishop's as feminine is, however, dangerously reductive, partly because poetic views of nature cannot be divided in terms of gender. In the case of Bishop, it must be emphasized that there is a long tradition, reaching back through the Romantics to Virgil's pastoral poetry, of writing about the less noble aspects of the natural world. What I want to argue, and you may disagree, is that 'Pike' exhibits a rather programmatic representation of nature; 'The Fish', in complete contrast, seems to be a continually shifting and open dialogue with it.

Bishop's sense of historical knowledge

ACTIVITY

Now please read 'At the Fishhouses' (in the Poetry Anthology).

'At the Fishhouses' is set in the maritime community of Bishop's childhood in Nova Scotia , a place and period of her life that became increasingly important in her poetry. Like 'The Fish', the emphasis seems to be on the description of a physical world, but the final part of the poem is markedly different from her characteristic style. In exploring the reasons for this, I want to concentrate on the implications of the final line of the poem: 'our knowledge is historical, flowing, and flown.'

DISCUSSION

The first stanza establishes the economy and livelihood of the fishing community as its subject ('We talk of the decline in the population /and of codfish and herring /while he waits for a herring boat to come in'). But Bishop has said that 'the last few lines of the first stanza of "At the Fishhouses" were also a *donnée* ... in a dream', and the realism of the description is offset by an emphasis on a timeless world (Stevenson, 1980, p.261). Look closely at the first six lines of the poem in particular: the work of the old man 'netting, /his net, in the gloaming almost invisible, /a dark purple-brown, /his shuttle worn and polished' is described in a visionary way. That ancient Anglo-Saxon word, 'gloaming' (meaning 'evening twilight'), sets us already in a dreamworld in which 'all is silver'. In the passage beginning 'The big fish tubs', 'beautiful herring scales' and 'iridescent flies' adhere to the fishermen's equipment, giving it an extraordinary aura (remember how the ordinary could become precious in 'The Fish'). The speaker's conversation with the old man ('He was a friend of my grandfather') establishes a bond with her own past and origins. In the final lines of this stanza, it is asserted that the value of tradition and labour symbolized by the old man has an even greater power than the aesthetic beauty to which he is apparently indifferent: 'He has scraped the scales, the principal beauty, /from unnumbered fish with that black old knife, /the blade of which is almost worn away.'

The second, transitional stanza moves us towards the sea-water; the third stanza establishes a different tone. Heaney describes this movement towards the astonishing force of the final lines as 'the slow-motion spectacle of a well-disciplined poetic imagination being tempted to dare a big leap, hesitating, and then with powerful sureness actually taking the leap' (Heaney, 1988, p.105). Here we enter a world that is not simply perilous ('element bearable to no mortal') but definitive, as emphasized by the repetition of 'Cold dark deep and absolutely clear'. In this third stanza, Bishop is quick to define the sensation of ultimate knowledge which the sea yields as different from a purely religious experience. She achieves this through a wry humour. The comical interchange with the seal is based on a pun which plays off what she enjoys singing ('Baptist hymns') against the total immersion which both she and the seal enjoy, and which is central to the Christian ritual of baptism. It's important to note that despite vestiges of her non-conformist upbringing – 'I'm full of hymns' (1984, p.xiii) – Bishop was, in religious terms, close to the position she described in one of her poems, 'The Unbeliever'. Her gentle irony at the expense of Christianity , evident in the lines, 'a million Christmas trees stand /waiting for Christmas', shows how she distances herself from a religious idiom to describe her sense of human knowledge.

Nevertheless, it is important to establish why she so elaborately and honestly exposes the metaphorical status of her meditation in the final lines of the poem ('*If* you should dip your hand in...', 'It is *like* what we imagine'). The dramatic change of tone begins with the four lines beginning 'I have seen it over and over'. Note the cumulative effect of the repetition of the description of the sea swinging 'above the stones' onto the shore; 'icily free above the stones, /above the stones and then the world'. This icy freedom, imagined to the touch and taste to 'burn', 'is like what we imagine knowledge to be':

> dark, salt, clear, moving, utterly free,
> drawn from the cold hard mouth
> of the world, derived from the rocky breasts
> forever, flowing and drawn, and since
> our knowledge is historical, flowing, and flown.

'Knowledge', the human activity associated in the Bible and in Milton's *Paradise Lost* with evil and with a male prerogative, is here imagined to emanate from a feminine and maternal body. But this is not the soft pastoral nature of literature and art – these are 'rocky breasts'; rather we are returned to the timeless world of human labour and endeavour in the first part of the poem. Just as the sea's movements are known, so knowledge is drawn from 'the cold hard mouth /of the world, derived from the rocky breasts / forever'. But so also 'since /our knowledge is historical', that is, we change and are changed, it is not simply 'flowing and drawn' but 'flowing, and flown'. The absolute clarity of the sea-water acknowledges time too.

Gender and identity

9.5 In an essay written in 1961, Bishop describes with humour and compassion the experience of being taken from her maternal grandparents in Nova Scotia to live with her paternal grandparents back in Worcester, Massachusetts where she had been born:

> I had been brought back unconsulted and against my wishes to the house my father had been born in, to be saved from a life of poverty and provincialism, bare feet, suet puddings, unsanitary school slates, perhaps even from the inverted *r's* of my mother's family. With this surprising extra set of grandparents, until a few weeks ago, no more than names, a new life was about to begin.
>
> (1984, p.17).

9.6 In fact, her stay in her grandparents' house was not a happy one and after a period of illness she spent the rest of her childhood and adolescence living with an aunt in Boston. But in this prose piece she remarks, 'Three great truths came home to me during this stretch of my life, all hard to describe and equally important' (ibid., p.31). The first, the falsity and power of sentimentality, and the second, consciousness of social status, are neither as remarkable as the third, her recognition of her own identity:

> After New Year's, Aunt Jenny had to go to the dentist, and asked me to go with her. She left me in the waiting room, and gave me a copy of the *National Geographic* to look at. It was still getting dark early, and the room had grown very dark. There was a big yellow lamp in one corner, a table with magazines, and an overhead chandelier of sorts. There were others waiting, two men and a plump middle-aged lady, all bundled up. I looked at the magazine cover – I could read most of the words – shiny, glazed, yellow and white. The black letters said: FEBRUARY 1918. A feeling of absolute and utter desolation came over me. I felt ... *myself* . In a few days it would be my seventh birthday. I felt *I, I, I,* and looked at the three strangers in panic. I was *one* of them too, inside my scabby body and wheezing lungs. 'You're in for it now,' something said. How had I got tricked into such a false position? I would be like that woman opposite who smiled at me so falsely every once in a while. The awful sensation passed, then it came back again. 'You are you', something said. 'How strange you are, inside looking out. You are not Beppo [her dog], or the chestnut tree, or Emma [her friend], you are *you* and you are going to be *you* forever'. It was like coasting downhill, this thought, only much worse, and it quickly smashed into a tree. *Why* was I a human being?
>
> (1984, pp.32–3)

ACTIVITY

Now please read 'In the Waiting Room' in the Poetry Anthology (you will remember the potential for momentous events to occur in waiting rooms from 'Revelation', and it is perhaps more than a coincidence that O'Connor was much admired by Bishop).

(a) In what major respects does the treatment of the incident in the poem (first published in 1971) differ from the prose account?

(b) How is the question of the child's identity related to the issue of the perception of other cultures, and to the issue of gender?

DISCUSSION

(a) What is most noticeable about the prose account is that it avoids detailed attention to the photographic images in the *National Geographic*. It also seems that the problem of identity in the prose account is perceived in relation to the other people in the waiting-room rather than to issues of gender and cultural difference as in the poem. It is significant that 'In the Waiting Room' was published as the first poem in *Geography III* (the title of the volume, and the epigraph in the form of a set of questions beginning *'What is Geography?'*, are taken from a late nineteenth-century geography textbook for schoolchildren).

(b) So how does the experience in the waiting-room relate to the issue of the representation of other cultures? First, the *National Geographic* is a celebrated example of magazine journalism which mediates ethnocentric North American perceptions about non-Western societies, hinted at in the reference to cannibalism in the caption 'Long pig'. In her reaction – 'Their breasts were horrifying' – the child reads beyond the cultural distortions of the photograph, seeing instead a distortion of something basic to human beings, their bodies, which her own aunt (and implicitly those well-clad occupants of the waiting-room) is all too willing to hide and disguise. The compelling power of the image creates two distinct reactions which seem to fuse into one cry of horror in the aunt and the child, one arising out of propriety, the other out of uninhibited anguish.

What is important is that the child is alienated from what her cry of horror inadvertently shares in, the identity of the rest of the people in the waiting room: 'you are one of *them*. /*Why* should you be one, too?' This environment is, then, as alien as that of the photographs in the *National Geographic*, and the child seems to see through the cultural imposition of Otherness into a repression of feminine sexuality.

This moment of horror and recognition describes something of Freud's definition of the 'uncanny', where the most familiar experience becomes the most strange and alien. In Lacanian terms, the symbolic order into which the child is propelled is, it seems, an arbitrary one and is perceived as such: 'What similarities ... held us all together /or made us all just one? /How – I didn't know any /word for it – "how unlikely"...' The child interrogates and exposes that symbolic order by which gender (and culture) are defined.

Women and madness

ACTIVITY

Please now read 'In the Village' in the Prose Anthology, pages 132–55.

9.7 Eight months after her birth, Elizabeth Bishop's father died, and her mother, who persisted in wearing black (as the story shows) for several years afterwards, suffered a series of mental breakdowns for which she was treated unsuccessfully. Elizabeth was taken to live with her maternal grandparents in Great Village, Nova Scotia. 'In the Village', first published in 1953, describes the return of her mother to her family there. After the final breakdown, which occurred when Elizabeth was five, her mother was put in a sanatorium and Elizabeth never saw her again.

9.8 In the American edition of her collection *Questions of Travel* (which is divided into two parts, entitled 'Brazil' and 'Elsewhere'), 'In the Village' appeared at the opening of the second part, followed by some poems about her childhood in Nova Scotia. It was the only prose piece in the collection.

9.9 The fear of madness as an issue in women's writing, and as an issue in the relation of gender to genre, is something Dinah Birch has alerted you to in the introduction to this block. It is significant to note that Bishop chooses to write about this intensely private and painful childhood experience in the form of prose rather than poetry, but also that she places the piece in a collection of poems. Those features of the piece which are intensely 'poetic' – for example, the passage from the description of the scream to the fitting of the mother's dress (pp. 132–5), and the last section in which the scream is subsumed within the sounds of the blacksmith's work (pp.154–5) – are so because of the skill of the narrative technique. Ellipsis and symbol (for example, the italicized *Clang* of Nate, the blacksmith) are used to authenticate the sense of a child displacing her emotions.

9.10 Juxtaposed with this is a realist, authentic note, true to a child's memory and emotional sophistication in her ability to distance herself from pain even while vulnerable to it. The description of taking Nelly to the pasture is as comical and as powerful as the moments of high drama, the fitting of the dress and the fire, with which it is interweaved.

9.11 I would like you to think about the narrative technique in two passages, the first from pages 132–5 and the second, the final part of the story on pages 154–5.

9.12 The interwoven themes of that final paragraph of 'In the Village' serve, perhaps, as a fitting conclusion to your brief study of Elizabeth Bishop. The detailed fidelity to memory and place gives even the most nondescript objects an individual beauty, 'the tin cans that glint there, brown and gold' (p.154). The sound of Nate shaping a horseshoe, *'Clang'*, strikes the note which echoes throughout the story, yet here it combines with the *'Slp'* of the river, to efface the haunting sound of the scream and the memories associated with it. As in 'At the Fishhouses', nature has a voice, 'It is the elements speaking: earth, air, fire, water', but human labour is equally affirmative and restoring, 'Nate! / Oh, beautiful sound, strike again!'.

10 *Adrienne Rich*

10.1 Adrienne Rich was born in Baltimore, on the East Coast of the USA, in 1929. She came from a middle-class Jewish background: her mother was a composer, her father a doctor. It looked at first as though her life would conform to the aspirations of her family. She graduated from Radcliffe, a prestigious women's college in 1951, and in 1953 married an economist at Harvard. They had three sons. Her identity as a poet, which she successfully combined with that of a wife and mother, seemed to confirm her wish to succeed within the terms of a male-dominated establishment. In 1951, the year of her graduation, her first book *A Change of World* was chosen for the Yale Younger Poets Award by W.H. Auden. He remarked with memorable condescension that 'the poems a reader will encounter in this book are neatly and modestly dressed, speak quietly but do not mumble, respect their elders but are not cowed by them, and do not tell fibs'.

10.2 As things turned out, the title of Adrienne Rich's first collection was more prophetic than Auden might have supposed. Her own world underwent radical change, and she began to want to change the worlds of others. She left her husband and started an academic career in New York. She also began an active political life, working for civil rights and anti-war movements throughout the 1960s, and publicly proclaiming her allegiance to feminist and lesbian organizations. In 1974 she was awarded the National Book Award for her collection *Diving Into the Wreck*. She rejected the award as a personal honour, then accepted it, in a statement written jointly with Alice Walker and Audre Lorde, black women writers who had also been nominated for the prize, 'in the name of all the women in a patriarchal world, and in the name of those who, like us, have been tolerated as token women in this culture, often at great cost and in great pain'. The poetry and criticism that Adrienne Rich has since published reflect the continuing development of her political identity as a lesbian feminist, and she has become one of the most influential figures within the women's movement in the USA.

10.3 The title poem of her third volume, *Snapshots of a Daughter-in-Law* (1963), begins to explore the new thinking leading to these profound changes in Adrienne Rich's life. Angels bear unexpected messages to a woman doing housework: *'Have no patience'*, *'Be insatiable'*, *'Save yourself; others you cannot save'*. Rich perceives that freedom will not be won without severity. She repudiates the standards by which women have been judged: 'slattern thought styled intuition /every lapse forgiven' ('Snapshots of a Daughter-in-Law', 1958–60). Adrienne Rich began her work as a feminist poet with the conviction that the woman poet must be 'more merciless to herself than history'.

10.4 As she continued to write, she began to think of history in different terms, devoting herself to the work of identifying and proclaiming a woman's literary tradition buried within a patriarchal past. You have already encountered her argument for the excavation of women's writing, in a brief passage from the introduction to her book *On Lies, Secrets, and Silence: selected prose 1966–1978* (1979, see Section 1). But it isn't simply literary history that Adrienne Rich is thinking of. She begins her foreword by recalling the lives of two American feminist activists of the nineteenth century, Elizabeth Cady Stanton (1815–1902) and Susan B. Anthony (1820–1906). Fellow workers and friends, these women shared half a century of commitment to reform. Adrienne Rich's point is that women's strength is revealed when they choose to live and work together:

> In October 1902, Elizabeth Cady Stanton died at the age of eighty-seven. Susan B. Anthony had worked with her for fifty years. Together, they learned the meaning of activism in the abolitionist movement. Together, over the cradles of Stanton's seven children, they had hammered out political strategy and speeches; together they had travelled from town to town organizing suffrage meetings; together had faced abuse and indignation, caricature and slander; together had argued, disagreed, and persevered through the bonds of an unremitting love and loyalty. Anthony, bereaved both of her most intimate friend and her most trusted colleague, found herself on Stanton's death besieged by reporters, whose questions revealed how little they knew and understood of the movement she and Stanton had labored in for half a century. Her cry of impatience could strike a chord of recognition in radical feminists today: *How shall we ever make the world intelligent on our movement?*
>
> (Rich, 1979)

10.5 The wish to make the world intelligent on her movement is what drives Adrienne Rich's poetry. In 1978, the year in which she wrote this paragraph, she published a volume of poetry called *The Dream of a Common Language*. In these poems she ponders 'the earth deposits of our history', considering the possibilities of life shared and communicated among women:

> I will not be divided ... from her or from myself
> by myths of separation
>
> ('Splittings', 1978)

10.6 Her life with the West Indian poet Michelle Cliff enabled Adrienne Rich to write with great tenderness about a physical love between women in this volume. She speaks of

> the homesickness for a woman, for ourselves
> ...
> two women, eye to eye
> measuring each other's spirit, each other's
> limitless desire,
> a whole new poetry beginning here.
>
> ('Transcendental Etude', 1977)

10.7 In 'Natural Resources' (1977), Rich develops the image of women as miners, revealing and reconstituting the 'natural resources' which sustain life. The poem (and the collection) is marked not only by an insistence on the need for women to learn to talk and listen to each other, expressing their memories and hopes in a common language, but also by a declared rejection of the hope that men might come to share this imagined world of mutual understanding and support. 'Natural Resources' has become widely known as an overt statement of Rich's separatist position. Controversially, she proclaims a feminism that would exclude men:

> the phantom of the man-who-would-understand,
> the lost brother, the twin -
> for him did we leave our mothers,
> deny our sisters, over and over?

'Culture and anarchy'

10.8 Rich's next collection, *A Wild Patience Has Taken Me This Far* (1981), develops the idea of a community of women, transcending time and place in its shared ideals and desires. 'Culture and Anarchy', reprinted from this collection, appears in the Poetry Anthology. The title of the poem refers to Matthew Arnold, who in 1869 published a powerful critique of Victorian society which he called *Culture and Anarchy*. But Arnold, who was pursuing balance and order in a way that gave scant attention to the situation and contribution of women, understood these concepts very differently from Adrienne Rich.

ACTIVITY

The experience of nineteenth-century women lies at the heart of 'Culture and Anarchy'. It is a long and complex poem, and I want to give some detailed attention to its structure and language. Could you turn to it now? Read the first two sections, as far as 'The all-alone feeling will creep over me...'. How do these sections relate to each other?

DISCUSSION

Your first feeling may have been that they are completely different, as though belonging to separate poems. The first begins reflectively, evoking a day in late summer. It soon becomes clear that the escaped daylilies and sharply angled light refer to more than themselves: Rich is writing about an escaped life moving towards ripeness (she was 52 years old when the poem was published). It is a life that contains domesticity and writing (typing at the kitchen table), communication with others (heaped up letters) and political activism (pamphlets on rape, forced sterilization). It also includes the remembered past. The snapshot of the Alabama woman 'still quilting in her nineties' leads into the title of a book, *The Life and Work of Susan B. Anthony*. Rich has always been something of an academic poet, writing out of a belief that historical research can provide food for her most creative work. Here she pays tribute to the scholarship that goes hand-in-hand with her poetry: the three-volume life of Susan Anthony she refers to was published in 1969, when feminist scholarship was still establishing its credentials. The memory of Susan Anthony and her lifelong friend Elizabeth Cady Stanton is, as we've seen, important to Adrienne Rich, representing a nurturing continuity of feminist life and work.

The second section of the poem, separated typographically from the first, moves into a different voice: that of Susan Anthony herself. A different voice – but not an alien one? Would you agree that the life suggested here is comparable to that sketched in the opening section of the poem? It too is compounded of domestic activity and political work, and supported by the writing and the companionship of other women. I wonder whether you recognized the references? Harriet Tubman was a black woman born a slave in 1821; having escaped to Philadelphia, she helped to establish the 'underground railway' on which hundreds of runaway slaves went to freedom in the northern states and Canada. She became a prominent member of the abolitionist and women's rights movements. During the Civil War she worked as cook, scout and spy for the Union army. Mrs Browning is more likely to be a familiar name to you: Elizabeth Barrett Browning (Adrienne Rich refers to her as Elizabeth Barrett elsewhere in the poem) was a distinguished poet, widely known for her reforming views. Despite these supportive presences, the section ends with a statement of solitude, an 'all-alone-feeling' that creeps over Anthony – and Rich too?

10.9 The juxtaposition of these two sections establishes a rhythm for the poem as a whole, as the present is seen to coexist with a remembered and supportive past. The 'all-alone feeling' is countered by an acknowledged commitment to a shared life that makes 'Culture and Anarchy' in part a love poem. But it is a love poem that contains more than a celebration of an individual relationship. It is crowded with names of the women who pioneered the beliefs that motivate Adrienne Rich's work, women whose names and words are woven into her text.

ACTIVITY

Could you now complete your reading of the poem? As you read, think about the following questions:

(a) Adrienne Rich has been accused of failing to 'resist the temptation to sloganize' (Margaret Atwood). How would you summarize the arguments for and against such a judgement of 'Culture and Anarchy'? Is it a sloganizing poem?

(b) The poem speaks of returning to 'my dream of a common language'. How far (if at all) would you say Rich's dream may be compared with Cixous's vision of *écriture féminine*?

DISCUSSION

(a) If we define 'sloganizing' as an aggressive promotion of a particular political viewpoint, then it's clear that elements of 'Culture and Anarchy' might answer the description. Though varied in its texture, 'Culture and Anarchy' contains passages where the primary business of the language is to convey an argument ('the strongest reason /for giving women all the opportunities...'). This is not a poem concerned with the delicately balanced presentation of alternative points of view. It is fired by a message, which it communicates with insistent force.

And the position advocated in the poem is, after all, a hard-hitting one. Rich alludes to the monumental *History of Woman Suffrage*, collaboratively edited by Elizabeth Stanton, Susan Anthony and Matilda Gage (1881–86). In her dream it becomes *The History of Human Suffering*, 'borne, /tended, soothed, cauterized /stanched, cleansed, absorbed, endured /by woman'. Women might be used to being silently omitted from the history of humanity, but it's not something that has usually happened to men. The effect is startling, as an academic history of women's protracted struggle for the vote merges into an image of the long history of human suffering 'like bound back issues of a periodical /stretching for miles'. Is it a justifiable fusion, do you think – or did you feel that Rich was sloganizing here?

Did you find elements in the poem that work in other ways? One important point I'd want to note is the poem's concern with a context in the natural world. Like many radical American feminists, Rich accepts – with worrying readiness, perhaps? – an idealized form of the traditional concept that women are more closely associated with nature and the natural than men. The forces of nature are seen here as anarchic, threatening our ordered perceptions with an uncontrollable fecundity rising from the earth ('Anarchy of August: as if already /autumnal gases glowed in darkness underground /the meadows roughen'). These energies are associated with the repressed strengths of women that are the poem's central concern. The woodpod swells to bursting and the stillness builds to thunder; so women's aspirations find 'power, release' in a breaking storm. In associating the recurrent images of emancipation in the poem with natural processes, Rich moves her argument and her language away from the specifics of any given historical moment. Political leaflets, the poem reminds us, are as transient as spiders' webs in wet grass: only the forces which give rise to them are permanent.

Another point that strikes me as significant here is the poem's preoccupation with the cadences of a settled domestic life. Rich writes about working in the kitchen as well as at the typewriter: her friend goes down to the garden to pick chard (a summer leaf vegetable); she slices beetroot. To write of these things may be interpreted as a feminist gesture, a way of celebrating work that, like the art of quilting petticoats, has long been unvalued. But it is hardly the technique of the slogan. In so far as the slogan can be termed a literary form, it has to do with public issues and public campaigns. For all its political drive, 'Culture and Anarchy' seems to me in many ways an intimate, private poem. Would you agree? Indeed, this is part of its point – remember the feminist wish to claim that 'the personal is the political' (see Section 1). The 'common language' of the poem leads to the possibility of a fulfilled 'solitude of self', and thence to the contentedly shared life affirmed in concluding lines which belong both to the past and present: 'we are one in aim and sympathy /and we should be together…'

(b) How much do you think this shared language has in common with Cixous's *écriture féminine*? There is at least one important respect in which it is different. Cixous, you'll remember, claimed that *écriture féminine* was not confined to women. Though it is more likely that women will express themselves in the way she describes, men (Shakespeare, for instance) might also have the capacity to do so (see Section 3). But Rich's lesbian separatism closes this option. She asserts that her 'common language' is shared between women; men have no part in it. Is this a sustainable claim, do you think? After all, publishing the poem means that all, male or female, are free to read it. And many men have been moved by it.

Other differences between Rich and Cixous may have struck you. On the evidence of 'Culture and Anarchy', it seems that Rich is less interested in fracturing the surface of logical discourse than Cixous. Her poetry (and prose) is measured and controlled, without the exclamatory, punning rush of words that we find in Cixous's exhortatory writing. Though what Rich is saying is often, as we've seen, contentious, the way in which she says it seems very much less unfamiliar, less innovatory than Cixous's iconoclastic prose.

Despite these distinctions, you might have noted many points at which Cixous and Rich work with shared assumptions. Both are products (and instigators) of reform in the world of higher education. It's important to notice that though Cixous and Rich want to speak on behalf of all women, both are prestigious figures within academic communities, and both write with the assumption that their readers will be able to respond to references of a scholarly kind. Both are passionately concerned with the dream of a woman's language. Though they produce it differently, both see such language at the heart of their hopes for a world in which the divisions of gender might be less repressive. Both want to use such language to change the rigid oppositions at the heart of our cultural constructions of gender. Both want to see interpretations of history that will refuse the primacy of masculine belligerence and competitiveness. Above all, both want to find ways to enable more women to listen to themselves and each other. Much seems to divide their standpoints, but they are united by the urgency of their wish to hear women breaking their silence.

11 New fictions: Toni Morrison's 'Song of Solomon'

11.1 Have we now arrived at a point where we can chart the association between language and gender? Not entirely. It's hard to imagine writers more different than the four poets you've just been reading, and their diversity is a vivid reminder that the issues we've been pondering can't be summed up in any simple way. Every writer, or speaker, has an individual position to express. But this distinctiveness defines itself against a broader framework of presuppositions, aspirations or anxieties. No one can wholly escape the web of deep-rooted cultural assumptions that feminist thinking has exposed. Our perceptions and imperceptions about language and gender are part of an ordered model for social relations which influences every aspect of our lives. In this sense our understanding of the issues must take on a political identity, for they are related to the ways in which human beings want to assume control over each other. Throughout the course, you have learned that language is always more than a transparent medium of communication. The black writer June Jordan puts the point succinctly in her essay 'White English/Black English: the politics of translation': 'The problem is that we are saying *language*, but really dealing with power' (Jordan, 1989, p.35).

11.2 In this section, we will be studying a novel deeply preoccupied with power. Much of the energy of Toni Morrison's *Song of Solomon* (1977) arises from a sharp sense of anger at the double burden visited upon those who are neither white nor male, in a culture in which power is overwhelmingly invested in both whiteness and masculinity. This novel examines what it means to be black, and female, in twentieth-century America. But Toni Morrison is also concerned with what goes into the making of black American men. The issues of gender and race are closely associated in her fiction. Morrison's writing weaves patterns in which all her characters – male and female, young and old, rich and poor, powerful and powerless – are irrevocably bound together.

11.3 *Song of Solomon* is the story of a family with both a private and public past, a mixed legacy which forms their identity as black people with a culture of their own. The threads of connection between its members reach back into the lost memories encoded in language – or languages, for Toni Morrison never loses sight of the multiple ways in which our speech carries its meaning. In *Song of Solomon*, the inheritance of power turns out to be a matter of words.

11.4 Our central aim in this section will be to consider some of the links between language and gender suggested by *Song of Solomon*. But other prominent themes will emerge as we investigate this rich and intricate book. You will discover that your thinking about the issues of earlier parts of the course – notably those of literature and ideology (Block 4), and of the development of new literatures in English (Block 6) – will be furthered by your work on *Song of Solomon*. Your own reading of the novel might well uncover themes or connections left unmentioned in my commentary. You might also find that your response to *Song of Solomon* changes significantly as you get to know it better. If it does, all to the good. You will discover that this is a book that abundantly rewards repeated reading, both of the text as a whole and of individual passages.

ACTIVITY

Before proceeding any further with this section, I would like you to read *Song of Solomon* carefully to the end of the first part (p.217 in your set text). You might choose to read the whole novel now, but I won't assume that you have at this stage. As you read, make some preliminary notes on the following questions:

(a) How does Toni Morrison challenge traditional concepts of the relationship between men and women in the first part of *Song of Solomon*?

(b) What do you notice about the treatment of time in this part of the novel? In answering this question, you might find it helpful to turn back to Dennis Walder's discussion of the functions of time as an aspect of narrative discourse in Block 2 Section 3.

Don't, however, feel constrained to limit your observations to these questions. Their function is to help you to focus your initial response.

DISCUSSION

(a) One of the most fundamental insights to emerge from contemporary theories of gender is that concepts of masculinity and femininity are separate from the biological divisions of sex (see Section 1). In thinking about the dealings between men and women in the first part of the novel, one point that might have struck you is that attributes of gender are seen to be shared between the sexes. I'd like to suggest that this is particularly true for Pilate and Milkman, characters whose relationship becomes central to the novel. Pilate is undoubtedly a woman; Milkman, just as clearly, is a man. But Pilate, physically strong, capable of aggression (most memorably when she deals with Reba's violent lover, pp.96–8) and vigorously in control of her life, displays many characteristics usually seen as masculine. Similarly, Milkman might be seen to show features traditionally understood to be feminine. Throughout the first part of the novel, he is as passive as Pilate is active. Fed beyond babyhood at his mother's breast, Milkman acquires a name suggesting a partial identification with femininity. Pilate's name, too, is ambivalent in its gender, for the biblical Pilate is, of course, a man. The weighted significance of names throughout the novel is a point we will return to.

If Milkman has elements of femininity in his character, just as Pilate has elements of masculinity, that doesn't stop him taking advantage of the privileged position that his maleness ('that hog's gut that hangs down between your legs', as Lena contemptuously puts it, p.215) gives him within a family in which the status of women (Ruth, Lena, First Corinthians) is low. Would you agree that the first part of the novel contains a strong element of feminist protest? Toni Morrison never forgets the patterns of oppression that have permitted black men to exploit the women they live with. I would point to Lena's assault on Milkman's unthinking selfishness, resulting in his leaving the family home and embarking on the voyage of discovery that constitutes the second part of the novel (pp.212–17), as the culmination of this aspect of the novel's anger. It is a trenchant reminder of how much Morrison owes to the tradition of feminist analysis of social inequality that has been so powerful in North America (see Section 10).

Another point that might have struck you about the relations between men and women in this part of the novel is Toni Morrison's scant interest in romance, that traditional staple of women's fiction in the Western world. We don't hear much in *Song of Solomon* about young people finding marriage partners for themselves. The relationship between Milkman and Hagar is a sterile one, while Corinthians and Porter represent a curiously elderly pair of lovers. My own feeling is that Morrison is more interested in what men and women of different generations might have to give each other – particularly with what the older woman might have to give a young man. Milkman, in a slow process of growth and education which continues throughout both parts of the novel, is again and again supported and taught by older women: Ruth, Lena, and most tellingly, Pilate.

What is Milkman taught by Pilate? How to boil an egg (you might like to try the recipe); how to look at colour; how to make wine. He is also taught how to speak. Did you notice that when Guitar and Milkman first visit Pilate's house, Pilate insists that he sharpens up his language? '"What kind of word is that?"… Her voice was light but gravel-sprinkled' (p.41). This is another of the ways in which Pilate might be seen to disrupt expectations about gender identity, for an emphasis on a hard-edged logical clarity in language is not, as we have seen, traditionally associated with femininity.

But the most important thing that Pilate has to teach Milkman is a sense of the past. The bond between men and women with a shared history is the foundation of the community and communication that have the potential to sustain Morrison's characters. Neither men nor women (perhaps with the partial exception of Pilate herself, the most isolated character in the novel?) are able to thrive alone, and a common knowledge of the past is what draws them together.

(b) You could have assembled a variety of notes under the general heading of the functions of time within the first part of *Song of Solomon*, for this is a novel centrally concerned with the need to construct meaning from memory. Time seems to move on different levels within the text. Perhaps you noted, for instance, that the novel begins with a very particular moment ('At 3.00pm on Wednesday the 18th of February, 1931...'). But the opening pages also refer, in the words of Pilate's song, to an undefined mythical past, in which flight was possible:

> Sugarman done fly away
> Sugarman done gone
> Sugarman cut across the sky
> Sugarman gone home

The lives of individuals, of families, of communities and of peoples coalesce within the scope of the buried history which becomes the focus in the second part of the novel, where we learn more about the 'sugarman' of Pilate's song. *Song of Solomon* persistently exploits a complex sense of time, looking forwards and backwards in ways which, in Genette's terms, unsettle the 'most basic forms of narration' (see Block 2 Section 3). But its concern with time is more than an abstract or even aesthetic preoccupation. I would argue that it is part of the book's political argument.

In making this claim, I'm partly thinking of the feminist reclamation of forgotten histories which forms such an important part of Adrienne Rich's political thinking. The forms of memory make up the substance of *Song of Solomon*. But remembered history, in this book, is not a matter of archives, letters or printed documents. The novel is, of course, a printed text, yet in many ways it is distrustful of the written word. Excluded from education, the black people of Shalimar, and of Southside, leave few written records of the remembered past. Here you might find yourself recalling other fiction in which oral traditions, rather than written culture, are examined and valued: Achebe's *Things Fall Apart* is an example that you've studied recently. The writing that *does* go on in *Song of Solomon* tends to be either futile (the fatuous poetry of Michael-Mary Graham) or destructive (Milkman's pitiless letter to Hagar). The illiterate Jake writes only one word in his life – the name of his daughter Pilate, which she keeps by her as a talisman. The written word is peripheral to the culture of these black people. But that does not mean that they are without the linguistic means to recall their lives.

Song of Solomon remembers and celebrates languages other than the written. One of its most striking characteristics is the energy with which it moves between different kinds of language. The past is commemorated through a network of stories, names, gossip and song. This is clear in the opening pages, as we learn about the folk-memories that give Not Doctor Street its name, and begin to learn about the still deeper memories that lie behind the enigmatic words of the song that we first hear as Robert Smith makes his doomed attempt to fly. Ideas of song, of flight, of naming and of memory constitute the central themes of *Song of Solomon*. As we go on to look closely at the texture of the novel, we will examine the complexities of these themes in more detail. First, I would like you to complete your reading of it. The remainder of this section will assume that you have done this.

11.5 Before looking more carefully at the themes which draw the novel together, I want to give some attention to Toni Morrison's beliefs and identity as a novelist, and to the wider cultural context of her work. What kind of writer is Toni Morrison?

Toni Morrison

11.6 Toni Morrison was born in Lorain, Ohio (a North-Eastern state of the USA; Lorain is on the southern shore of Lake Erie, with Canada on the other shore), in 1931, the year in which *Song of Solomon* begins with Milkman's birth. Milkman's fictional development, from an unreflecting acceptance of an alien culture to a conscious search for roots of his own, is in part an expression of the changing values of Morrison's own generation. Toni Morrison has two children – both boys, a fact that gives her reason to be interested in what goes into the making of black men. She has been successful in more than one professional field: in addition to writing five novels to date (the first, *The Bluest Eye,* was published in 1970, and was followed by *Sula* (1974), *Song of Solomon* (1977), *Tar Baby* (1981), and *Beloved* (1987)), she has taught creative writing in several universities, and has worked as a senior editor with a large publishing house in New York. Her involvement with teaching and publishing is an important expression of a belief that she has always held: that the writer must be part of a community, not a sequestered talent working in isolation.

ACTIVITY

In her essay 'Rootedness: the ancestor as foundation' Toni Morrison comments on some of the links she sees between her work and that of other black North American writers. You will find this essay reprinted in the Reader (pp.326–32). Please read it now. How do you think her comments on the significant attributes of black writing in North American might relate to what she is attempting in *Song of Solomon*?

DISCUSSION

Toni Morrison begins her essay with an expression of regretful nostalgia for a time 'when an artist could be genuinely representative *of* the tribe and *in* it; when an artist could have a tribal or racial sensibility and an individual expression of it'. This she says is no longer viable, which is a reason for keeping her life 'as private as possible'. Nevertheless, her essay makes it clear that some approximation of what she has described – an art capable of expressing both individuality and communality – remains an important practical ideal for her work. Toni Morrison is suspicious of the idea of the singular hero or heroine. Similarly, she reacts against the notion that the artist is a heroic figure. In Morrison's account, the artist emerges as someone with a heavy responsibility towards the nurturing culture. Writing is fashioned from the past, and it has a duty to warn about the future. 'I want to point out the dangers, to show that nice things don't always happen to the totally self-reliant if there is no conscious historical connection. To say, see – this is what will happen.'

How, then, does Morrison see the writer expressing this sense of a rooted community? She singles out three methods as being of special importance, each of them associated with her perception of black art:

(a) One important element in her approach is the role of what she calls a 'chorus', defined here as a body of response or opinion other than that of the characters themselves. In *Song of Solomon,* this narrative function is undertaken by the 'neighbourhood or community that responds in the two parts of town'.

(b) Morrison also points to an emphasis on the spoken voice in her work. We have already noticed how her writing distances itself from the primacy of the written word: though her fiction inevitably consists of print ('only the letters of the alphabet and some punctuation', as Morrison briskly puts it), there is a persistent drive towards evoking the textures and rhythms of what the people she is interested in might say and how they might say it. This is an important part of Morrison's attempt to create a direct route of entry for the reader to participate in her writing. The spoken quality of her work refuses closure. We are invited to complete the books ourselves, as though in a conversation with an author.

Morrison's essay makes it clear that *Song of Solomon* is deliberately not a finished artefact. It awaits completion by the reader. This is an attribute clearly marked in the conclusion of the book, where the reader is, disconcertingly, not given a conventionally concluded plot ('it did not matter which of them would give up his ghost in the killing arms of his brother…'). But this openness is evident throughout the construction of the novel. Morrison comments:

> To make the story appear oral, meandering, effortless, spoken – to have the reader *feel* the narrator without *identifying* that narrator, or hearing him or her knock about, and to have the reader work *with* the author in the construction of the book – is what's important. What is left out is as important as what is there.
>
> (Reader, p.328)

Some of what Morrison is saying in this essay will have a familiar feel to you. This is not the first time you've encountered the idea of a kind of writing in which 'what is left out is as important as what is there'. Such a concept was, you'll recall, central to the tenets of Modernist thinking, and from this point of view Morrison's narrative procedures in *Song of Solomon* are not as different from those of Virginia Woolf in *Mrs Dalloway* (to take an example known to you from Block 2) as you might at first be inclined to imagine. More recent parallels might also suggest themselves to you (Samuel Beckett's *Endgame*? Muriel Spark's *The Prime of Miss Jean Brodie*?). Concepts of fragmentation and incompletion have continued to be important in the development of thinking about literature in many different ways. Toni Morrison has no wish to claim originality in her narrative devices: 'I am not suggesting that some of these devices have not been used before and elsewhere.' Her point is that she uses them in a particular way – a way that she sees as specifically related to the inherited culture of black people.

(c) A third aspect of this culture that Morrison considers particularly important in this essay is the idea of the ancestor, the embodiment of a past which she believes to be necessary to both the present and the future. Pondering ways in which other black writers – Ralph Ellison, Toni Cade Bambara, Henry Dumas, Richard Wright, James Baldwin – have treated the ancestor, Morrison reflects that here too absence might be as significant as presence: 'It was the absence of an ancestor that was frightening, that was threatening, and it caused huge destruction and disarray in the work itself.' Some of that destruction and disarray is reflected in the fictional lives of Milkman and his father – both searching for a validating ancestor, a figure they instinctively suppose to be male. Macon Dead ponders a family he finds unsatisfactory: 'Surely, he thought, he and his sister had some ancestor, some lithe young man with onyx skin and legs as straight as cane stalks, who had a name that was real' (p.23).

The discovery of Solomon's story is, in a sense, the fulfilment of Macon Dead's hunger for a forefather who could confer meaning and dignity on his life. Refusing slavery, Solomon flies back to Africa. His magically defiant disappearance gives Macon's son Milkman the image of liberation that he longs for. But Solomon is an ancestor whose message is one of ruthlessly chosen absence, for his mythical flight means the abandonment of his family. His example is qualified by others, for there is in this text, as Morrison reminds us in her essay, an ancestor who is not male, and who does not disappear: 'In *Song of Solomon* Pilate is the ancestor.'

Pilate's timelessness – an attribute signified by her lack of a navel, which seems to some extent to set her apart from the everyday world – makes her both a participant and a detached observer in the social life which surrounds her. Like Solomon, she is invested with magical strength. Carrying her father's bones with her without realizing it, Pilate is the means of making contact with the past. Her alienation is a source of power. But it is also, as Toni Morrison makes clear, a source of debility. Despite her function in the novel as an emblem of sustaining ancestorship, and despite her fierce love for her daughter and granddaughter, Pilate's isolation causes her to fail as a parent. Removed from the supportive social framework she needs, Pilate's daughter Reba loses the capacity to form solid relationships with those outside her immediate family. As a result, she can create no satisfactory bond with the men who drift in and out of her life. Pilate's granddaughter Hagar, still further removed from a community that might have helped her, is fatally disabled by this withdrawal; though the protective devotion of her mother and her grandmother surrounds her from birth, she is destroyed by her obsessive love for Milkman. Here the novel speaks most clearly as a warning. To be cut off from the community which gave rise to our lives, no matter how painful the history of that community, is to enact a species of self-destruction of which Hagar's death is an extreme and pathetic expression.

How does the position outlined in 'Rootedness: the ancestor as foundation' relate to that of other North American women writers? One important point to note here is that Toni Morrison's firm commitment to the community and to the art of the community sets her at odds with feminist writers and critics who seek to celebrate a language of their own. What women have to say is given its full weight in *Song of Solomon*, but Morrison has no interest in a specifically or exclusively feminine discourse. Her vision of the language in which we might best speak to each other includes men:

> Pilate is the apogee of all that: of the best of that which is female and the best of that which is male and that balance is disturbed if it is not nurtured, and if it is not counted on and if it is not reproduced. That is the disability we must be on guard against for the future – the female who reproduces the female who reproduces the female. You know there are a lot of people who talk about the position that men hold as of primary importance, but actually it is if we don't keep in touch with the ancestor that we are, in fact, lost.
>
> (Reader, p.331)

It's worth recalling, at this point, Adrienne Rich's very different concept of the ways in which the past might be reconstructed. Rich is interested in the discovery and perpetuation of a specifically female past. Morrison also wishes to assert the role, often buried, that women have played in history. But she is suspicious of the idea that gender might be all-inclusive as a means of categorizing human experience. The ancestor, for Toni Morrison, is not to be defined by either masculinity or femininity.

One reason for this is that the images of race that construct our identity are, in Toni Morrison's eyes, as significant as the patterns of social division established through gender. Adrienne Rich's point is that in the flux of American society a sense of the past is hard to come by ('In America we have only the present tense', as she put it in her poem

'The Burning of Paper Instead of Children', 1968). Not being a man makes it more likely that you might view your history as either insignificant or impenetrable. Toni Morrison reminds us that not being white has a comparable effect. Would you agree that this condition of racial exclusion is not, in *Song of Solomon*, simply to be equated with being of African ancestry? Like many black North American writers (Alice Walker is an example), Toni Morrison associates the forgotten history of African slaves and their descendants with the forgotten history of the American Indian peoples. Pilate and Macon Dead have two parents. Their father, Jake, is a son of the African Solomon. But their mother, Sing, comes from an Indian family, her name an abbreviation of 'Singing Bird'. The heritage of the Dead family is half African-American, half native American. When the visiting ghost of Pilate's father speaks, he can only repeat the name of his dead Indian wife. Pilate interprets this as an expression of his wish that she should sing, and her response to his instruction becomes a saving force in her life. A further meaning, however, emerges from this echoed name, as Milkman's researches reveal more of his family's past. In repeating the word 'Sing', Jake, the first Macon Dead, is reminding Pilate of a lost part of her legacy. Her grandfather was a 'flying African', but her mother, too – 'Singing Bird' – could fly, though in a different way. Sing's roots are deep within the American land to which she returns in death, and to which Jake, too, is returned by his daughter, as the final act of her life. It is an act that enables Pilate to inherit the power of both her African father and her native American mother, as she too takes flight:

> Milkman laid her head down on the rock. Two of the birds circled round them. One dived into the new grave and scooped something shiny in its beak before it flew away.
>
> Now he knew why he loved her so. Without ever leaving the ground, she could fly.
>
> (p.336)

11.7 Reinterpreting roots, and looking for the past, places Toni Morrison within an important strand in the developing tradition of black women's writing in America. It is a tradition that always contains a sense of opposition, of writing against the grain – partly because the repression with which black women in a white culture have always been faced makes any kind of self-assertion an act of defiance, but also because the processes of writing and publication have seemed particularly out of tune with a culture that was for many years a matter of the spoken rather than the written word. Zora Neale Hurston (1901–60) was among the first and most compelling of the black women writers to rediscover and celebrate the oral forms of black culture that form such a significant part of *Song of Solomon*. Hurston was particularly interested in black folklore in the South of the USA, which she recorded and incorporated into a series of pioneering books, perhaps most successfully in her extraordinary novel *Their Eyes Were Watching God* (1937). But Hurston's insistence on the need to preserve black traditions prompted her to oppose moves towards social integration, and she became a deeply controversial and often unpopular figure among black writers of her day. More recently, positive aspects of her writing have been recognized and acclaimed by younger black women writers – notably the novelist Alice Walker, whose critical book *In Search of our Mother's Gardens* (1983) includes a sympathetic consideration of what Hurston contributed to the black women's literary movement, of which Walker herself is a prominent member. Hurston's fiction may be seen to address a question that dominates Toni Morrison's thought.

How is the identity of black culture, particularly the culture of the agricultural South, to be perpetuated in a changing world? The critic Susan Willis formulates this as the central issue of Morrison's work: 'The problem at the centre of Morrison's writing is how to maintain an Afro-American cultural heritage once the relationship to the black rural south has been stretched thin over distance and generations' (Willis, 1984, p.264).

11.8 Other black women have focused on the need to understand the implications of a collective past. Paule Marshall (b.1929) has written of the West Indian heritage shared by many blacks in North America: her *Brown Girl, Brownstone* (1951), concerning a Barbadian girl growing up in Brooklyn, was both innovative and influential. Toni Morrison's *Tar Baby* (1981) represents a very different treatment of this theme. Another forceful writer of Morrison's generation is Maya Angelou (b.1928), whose most widely read book, the autobiographical *I Know Why The Caged Bird Sings* (1970) deals with a hard childhood in the Southern States of the 1930s and 1940s, and, as its title suggests, prefigures some of the themes of Toni Morrison's fiction. Further volumes of autobiography and poetry have consolidated Angelou's reputation. Growing in numbers and assurance, these writers are conscious of working towards the construction of a literature of their own, and they are keenly aware of their own literary ancestry. The black women novelists, poets and critics (Gloria Naylor, Nikki Giovanni, Barbara Christian, and many others) who are continuing to change the map of American writing have been ready to pay tribute to the achievements of their literary ancestors, the black women whose work broke ground which is turning out to be fertile.

11.9 The point of enumerating these black women writers – my list is both cursory and selective – is not to suggest that they all write in the same way. They don't. Nor do they always display the same concerns. But they do write out of a body of common experiences and aspirations. Like Toni Morrison, they are often preoccupied with the ways in which forms of shared memory might support the search for identity and self-esteem. They are often keenly political in their ambitions; many have been involved in the American movement for civil rights and the associated black power struggle in the 1950s and 1960s. Like Morrison, all of these writers are intensely interested in the relationship between language and power.

11.10 The concerns of *Song of Solomon* do not, then, arise out of a cultural vacuum. For all her innovative drive, Toni Morrison is as alert to the authority of historical tradition as (say) her compatriot T.S. Eliot, though the tradition she reveres is a long way from Eliot's resonant phrases from St Augustine or Dante.

11.11 One of the primary ways in which her awareness of tradition is expressed in the novel is in its interest in the power of names. We have already given some attention to this aspect of the text. I want now to examine the names in *Song of Solomon* in more detail.

Naming

11.12 Critics have wanted to draw attention to one aspect of the significance of naming in *Song of Solomon*, and elsewhere in Toni Morrison's fiction: it can be seen to constitute a very specific link with an African perspective of her work. Barbara Christian points out that 'in African cosmology it is through *nommo*, the correct naming of a thing, that it comes into existence' (Christian, 1985, p.157). But it is clear that Toni Morrison invests her names with a range of associations and meanings that are not confined to those of African cosmology. Names are an expression of the sense of the many-sided history that she wants to communicate to her readers – as we are reminded in the novel's epigraph:

The fathers may soar
And the children may know their names

Did you notice the ambiguity in that epigraph? 'The children may know their names' – whose names? Their own, or their fathers? Primarily their fathers – but would you agree that the epigraph finally refers to both fathers and their children? In *Song of Solomon*, discovering the name of your departed father is a way of learning about yourself. Toni Morrison's first novels, *The Bluest Eye*, 1970 and *Sula*, 1974, focused on motherhood. In *Song of Solomon*, she continues to think about mothers – but here she also ponders fathers. You'll recall that the novel is dedicated to 'Daddy'.

11.13 We have already noticed that Pilate's name is derived from the Scriptures, chosen by her father according to the traditional custom of blind selection from the Bible. Her name, then, could be seen as an expression of a Christian heritage. But the biblical Pilate is – as the scandalized midwife reminds Jake – 'the man that killed Jesus' (p.24). Throughout the novel, Pilate stands for values that are deeply opposed to the concepts of humility and acceptance that are what she understands of the Christian faith. Only when she assumes a demeaningly subservient disguise in order to rescue Milkman and Guitar from the police station does she underpin her speech with reference to the authority of the Bible: 'Milkman was astonished. He thought Pilate's only acquaintance with the Bible was the getting of names out of it, but she quoted it, apparently verse and chapter' (p.207).

11.14 Feigning frailty in the interests of Milkman and Guitar, Pilate pretends that the bones which her nephew and his friend attempted to steal from her represent the remains of a lynched husband whom she calls Mr Solomon – 'she always called him Mr Solomon because he was such a dignified colored man' (p.207). In the second part of the novel, we learn that the man whose bones Pilate guards are actually those of her father, the father who gave her her name, and whose protective and guiding spirit had remained with her since his death. He was not called Solomon, but first Jake, and then, through the arbitrary misunderstanding of a drunken soldier, Macon Dead. Solomon is nevertheless a name of central significance in the part of history which Milkman slowly uncovers in the second part of the novel. It turns out to be the name of Jake's father, Pilate's grandfather, Milkman's great-grandfather: Solomon, the mysterious ancestral African who flew home.

11.15 Solomon becomes much more than a man's name. It is also the name of a place and its people, and of a song. The words that Pilate sings at Milkman's birth are echoed by the children that Milkman finds playing in the dust as he searches for the roots of the family. But they give Milkman a different version of the song, substituting the name 'Solomon' for 'Sugarman'. Milkman is to alter the words again when he returns the song to Pilate as she dies, and 'Sugarman' becomes 'Sugargirl'. This changing song is what gives the novel its name. It is the key that enables Milkman to unlock the enigma of his inheritance:

> Jay the only son of Solomon
>
> Come booba yalle, come...
>
> Everybody in this town is named Solomon, he thought wearily. Solomon's General Store, Luther Solomon (no relation), Solomon's leap, and now the children were singing '*Solomon* don't leave me' instead of '*Sugarman*'. Even the name of the town sounded like Solomon: Shalimar, which Mr Solomon and everybody else pronounced *Shalleemone*.
>
> (p.302)

11.16 This song of Solomon has, like Pilate's name, a direct association with the Bible. Did the title of the novel recall the Bible to you? One of the books of the Old Testament is in fact called 'The Song of Solomon'. But, like the

Christ-killing biblical Pilate, the biblical song of Solomon might well be seen to bear a mutinous relationship to the Christian religion. In the Old Testament, 'The Song of Solomon' is a lyrical celebration of the power of love between women and men – not a theme with which Christian doctrine has generally found it easy to come to terms with. Interestingly, this song of Solomon is the only book of the Bible to be called a song – and it is the only one in which the voice of a black woman is heard: 'I am black, but comely, O ye daughters of Jerusalem, as the tents of Kedar, as the curtains of Solomon' (The Song of Solomon 1:5).

11.17 No doubt you can think of other biblical references in the naming of characters in *Song of Solomon*, for the women of the Dead family have all been named in this way – though their names (Ruth, Magdalene, First Corinthians, Reba, Hagar) have none of the ambivalent implications of Pilate's namesake. But the Bible is not the only source of names in the novel. How are other characters named? According to disposition (Sweet), after frustrated ambitions (Guitar), misunderstandings (Macon Dead) or remembered incidents (Milkman). Guitar reflects bitterly on the haphazard way in which his people find their names: 'Niggers get their names the way they get everything else – the best way they can.' Guitar's repudiation of the significance of names ('I don't give a damn about names', p.162) suggests his profound and finally destructive alienation. But such processes are seen in a more positive light at the end of the novel. Milkman contemplates the naming of black men and women:

> Their names. Names they got from yearnings, gestures, flaws, events, mistakes, weaknesses. Names that bore witness. Macon Dead, Sing Byrd, Crowell Byrd, Pilate, Reba, Hagar, Magdalene, First Corinthians, Milkman, Guitar, Railroad Tommy, Hospital Tommy, Empire State (he just stood around and swayed), Small Boy, Sweet, Circe, Moon, Nero, Humpty-Dumpty, Blue Boy, Scandinavia, Quack-Quack, Jericho, Spoonbread, Ice Man, Dough Belly, Rocky River, Gray Eye, Cock-a-Doodle-Doo, Cool Breeze, Muddy Waters, Pinetop, Jelly Roll, Fats, Leadbelly, Bo Diddley, Cat-Iron, Peg-Leg, Son, Shortstuff, Smoky Babe, Funny Papa, Bukka, Pink, Bull Moose, B.B., T-Bone, Black Ace, Lemon, Washboard, Gatemouth, Cleanhead, Tampa Red, Juke Boy, Shine, Staggerlee, Jim the Devil, Fuck-up, and *Dat* Nigger.
>
> (p.330)

Such names may be bizarre, and not always dignified, but they are an exuberant expression of the stubborn individuality of a people that refuses to be crushed into uniformity. In this novel, only the Dead family bear a dispiriting name.

11.18 For Macon Dead, the head of this family, the chancing on unorthodox names is a source of irritation. The implications of his son's nickname are unpleasantly clear to him, though its origin is not:

> It was a matter that concerned him a good deal, for the giving of names in his family was always surrounded by what he believed to be monumental foolishness. No one mentioned to him the incident out of which the nickname grew because he was a difficult man to approach – a hard man, with a manner so cool it discouraged casual or spontaneous conversation.
>
> (p.15)

11.19 This hard coolness, excluding Macon Dead from the unruly but affectionate community which gave his son the name Milkman, makes the feminine implications of the word disturbing to him: 'It certainly didn't sound like the honest job of a dairyman, or bring to mind cold bright cans standing on the back porch, glittering like captains on parade. It sounded dirty, intimate, and hot.' Macon Dead has made his wealth at the expense of the latent femininity in his nature. As a boy, he had lovingly cared for the motherless Pilate. As a successful man, he despises Pilate and all she stands for, and is totally divided from every woman with whom he comes in contact. If Hagar's unhappy fate represents the dangers of a life which excludes men, Macon Dead is an expression of what can happen to those who excise femininity from their lives.

Places

11.20 Places are as important to the structure of the novel as names, and this is another dimension of the novel in which Toni Morrison expresses her awareness of the black cultural tradition that she wants to record and celebrate in *Song of Solomon*. Black people in America – like white people, though often in more painful circumstances – have been travellers, and their memories of places they have seen and moved on from is an important element in their sense of collective identity.

ACTIVITY

Before reading on, make notes on what seem to you the most significant ways in which the novel exploits a sense of place.

DISCUSSION

One very simple point to note here is that the basic design of the novel is determined by its sense of place. The first part takes place in the Northern states; the second traces Milkman's discoveries in the South. It was in the rural Southern states that Macon Dead worked with his father and cared for his sister, and it is in the rural South that his son Milkman is able to come to terms with the feminine element in his nature and with his family history. *Song of Solomon* pivots on the difference between the relatively prosperous Northern states of the US, dominated by what Morrison sees as the coldly materialistic values of white culture, and the poorer but more vital world of the South, where the Dead family had its origins. Generally speaking, the North represents the triumph of logic, fact and possession. Though its men are often violent and are as ready to assume a proprietary attitude towards their women as their Northern counterparts, the South is nevertheless a place that often seems to value other qualities: intuition, warmth, the power of emotion. Would it be feasible, do you think, to suggest that characteristics defined as feminine in the novel are broadly speaking located in the South? Or is that too simple a categorization?

Whatever your views on the ways in which the Northern and Southern states might be differentiated in terms of gender in *Song of Solomon*, it is clear that the novel assumes a different direction when it moves south. As if to underscore the difference, the second part of the novel takes us straight into the world of myth and fairytale: 'When Hansel and Gretel stood in the forest and saw the house in the clearing before them, the little hairs at the nape of their necks must have shivered.' Circe, unimaginably old and surrounded by her animal familiars, is the witch we all encountered as children. But she has ancestors in more than one world of magic, for she is also the Circe of Greek myth, the enchantress whose powers enable her to transform men into animals, pride into degradation.

The eclecticism of Morrison's sources is revealing. Clearly, her vision of the South has to do with more than geography. Neither ancient Greek myths nor the fairy stories of Northern Europe seem to be part of black culture. But they too deal with the irrational energies which in this novel find their home in the

Southern states. Morrison has a wide and varied academic background. Her knowledge includes a great deal more than what is specific to black culture, though she values nothing more highly. She confidently claims the cultural wealth of Europe as part of her inheritance as a black novelist – in a way that might be compared with Walcott's dynamic use of the literary inheritance of Europe in forging his own voice as a black poet. Just as being a woman ought not, in her argument, to insulate her from the experience of men, so being a black novelist does not exclude her from the use of fictional motifs from cultures that are not black.

I claimed that place is as important to the structure of the novel as names. You may have noticed that they are connected, for places in *Song of Solomon* sometimes acquire their names as eccentrically as people. The novel opens with the story of the naming of Not Doctor Street – a story which expresses the pride of black people, their resourcefulness, and their humour. It is part of the folklore of Southside, where the poor black people, most of them migrants from the Southern states (Louisiana, Virginia, Alabama, and Georgia), live. Again the name is significant, for the Southside folk maintain some of the vitality of the South in a cold Northern city. Other areas of the city are alien to this down-at-heel animation. The shops 'downtown' glitter with the promise of well-being and riches not to be found in Southside: 'Only downtown were the lights large, bright, festive, and full of hope.' The pleasures of Honoré Island – that 'niggerheaven' as Guitar fiercely puts it – are open to black people, but only if they have money. These are the people whose aspirations to property-owning wealth interest Macon Dead: 'in a few years – five or ten – a whole lot of coloreds will have enough to afford it. A whole lot.'

Macon Dead's willing assumption of the values of the North makes him determined to win the wealth by which he judges people. He does not hesitate to do so at the expense of his own people. His callous treatment of Guitar's grandmother causes him to reject the nurturing values associated with the poverty of the South in his mind: 'What's it gonna profit you, Mr Dead, sir, to put me and them children out?' The consequences of Macon Dead's behaviour in the North are visited upon his son in the South. Milkman's trip to Danville, Pennsylvania, and Shalimar (or Shaleemone, or Solomon), Virginia, is first prompted by what his father has infected him with: an infatuation with the idea of gold – though gold is not what he finally finds. It is when he hears about the plan to steal the gold that Guitar first calls Milkman 'My man' (p.176), the phrase with which he is later to pursue his friend in the mistaken belief that he has cheated him of the treasure. Guitar is not wholly wrong, for what Macon Dead and his son have come to represent in Guitar's mind is the force of greed and exploitation that did cheat him, years ago, destroying his father and condemning him to the deprived childhood which his name records. Guitar's murderous hunting of Milkman is the outcome of a sequence of events traced throughout the novel, linking different places and times in a complex network of meaning.

Flying

11.21 Toni Morrison sees the image of flight as a vital part of the novel's engagement with a specifically black culture. Soon after the publication of *Song of Solomon* in 1977, she spoke about what she had been trying to achieve in the novel:

> Flying is the central metaphor in 'Song' – the literal taking off and flying into the air, which is everybody's dream. My children [both boys] used to talk about it all the time – they were amazed when they found they couldn't fly. They took it for granted that all they had to do was jump up and flap

> their arms. I use it not only in the African sense of whirling dervishes and getting out of one's skin, but also in the majestic sense of a man who goes too far, whose adventures take him far away ... black men travel, they split, they get on trains, they walk, they move. I used to hear those old men talk about travelling – which is not getting from here to there, it's the process – they even named themselves after trains. It's part of black life, a positive, majestic thing, but there is a price to pay – the price is the children. The fathers may soar, they may triumph, they may leave, but the children know who they are; they remember, half in glory and half in accusation. That is one of the points of 'Song': all the men have left someone, and it is the children who remember it, sing about it, mythologize it, make it a part of their family history.
>
> (Watkins, 1977, p.50)

11.22 Toni Morrison makes it clear that flight, as it is conceived in *Song of Solomon*, is a gendered activity. Do you recall how the novel begins? It opens with an account of a man who wants to fly: 'The North Carolina Mutual Life Insurance agent promised to fly from Mercy to the other side of Lake Superior at three o'clock.' This is the event that precipitates the birth of Milkman: 'A little bird'll be here with the morning' (p.14). Taking wing is something that the men of the novel persistently want to do, leaving the women and children behind.

11.23 Here Morrison seems to think of flight very differently from Hélène Cixous, who writes in 'The laugh of the Medusa' of flying in specifically feminine terms. You may remember the passage: 'Flying is woman's gesture – flying in language and making it fly. We have all learned the art of flying and its numerous techniques; for centuries we've been able to possess anything only by flying...' (p.325 in the Reader). In the first part of the novel, it looks as though women want to have nothing to do with the aspiration to fly. Only Hagar, maddened by Milkman's dismissive letter, is seen in a disoriented and damaging version of the flight her lover longs for – 'spinning into a bright blue place where the air was thin and it was silent all the time...' (p.99). But in the second part of the novel, where we encounter memories of Sing Byrd and witness Pilate's final moments, we are led to realize that flight of a different kind might also be practised by the women of the novel, and that Cixous's comments do not conflict with the terms of *Song of Solomon* as decisively as we might have imagined.

11.24 The masculine wish for flight in the sense of escape is neither wholly celebrated nor wholly condemned by Toni Morrison. The men's restlessness, their refusal to be confined, is exhilarating. But it can also be seen as irresponsible. The mythical escape of the book's oldest ancestor, the flying African Solomon, is the founding memory of *Song of Solomon*. His flight was a fabulous getaway. But there was a price to pay. 'Who'd he leave behind?' asks Sweet, all too familiar with men's ways. He left behind twenty-one children, who could not get away. He also abandoned a wife, Ryna, who was driven to insanity by her loss, and whose weeping is remembered in the landscape (Ryna's Gulch, with its ghostly crying) which Solomon so magnificently spurned. Hagar is the descendant of Ryna: a woman who cannot live after her lover takes wing. If flight is irresponsible, her dependence proves to be inadequate. As so often, Pilate represents an equilibrium between opposing conditions: solidly independent and an eager traveller (you will remember her habit of collecting stones from the places she has seen), she is also completely loyal to the people who need her. Pilate is not interested in the kind of flight that involves leaving the earth behind: 'She wouldn't set foot on an airplane...'

11.25 In the uncertainty Toni Morrison creates about whether Solomon actually flew or not ('You know, like a bird. Just stood up in the fields one day, ran up some hill, spun round a couple of times, and was lifted into the air. Went right on back to wherever it was he came from.'), we see the challenging of realistic narrative which characterizes the novel as a whole. Men can't fly. Nor are women born without navels. Toni Morrison is fully aware of the questions this raises, and doesn't hesitate to remind her readers of them: 'Jesus! Here he was walking around in the middle of the twentieth century trying to explain what a ghost had done. But why not? he thought. One fact was certain: Pilate did not have a navel. Since that was true, anything could be, and why not ghosts as well?' (p.294). Throughout *Song of Solomon*, meticulously observed social detail is juxtaposed with events and observations that suggest a transcendence of the natural world. The reluctance to be bound by the conventions of a realistic representation of natural fact is a fictive strategy with a very long history: fairy stories, folk-tales, or ghost stories all depend on a concept of the supernatural, as do the ancient myths (African, Indian, American, Hebrew, Australian, European...) which constitute the oldest forms of narrative we have. The idea of flight is often central to these narratives: angels, fairies, goddesses and gods commonly have wings. We have already noticed some of the uses that Morrison makes of such fictional resources in *Song of Solomon*. In this, as in other innovative aspects of the book, she is not working in isolation. Many other novelists, including black writers both male and female (Alice Walker and Salman Rushdie are just two of the most prominent examples), who have been suspicious of the dominance of logic and fact rather than feeling and intuition in Western culture, have incorporated the supernatural resonance of popular narratives (fairy stories, or myths) into their novels.

11.26 Would you agree that this is a strategy associated, though not identical, with the novel's thinking about gender? Milkman hears the inspiring story of his great-grandfather's flight from a woman, Susan Byrd. Most of the supernatural occurrences in the book (the appearance of the ghost of Jake, the first Macon Dead, for instance – or the administration of the love potion which brings about Milkman's conception) have to do with Pilate, the character who comes closest to representing an ideal balance between the feminine and the masculine. Milkman's frustrated development, bound up with the poisoned relationship between his father and his mother, is suggested by the repeated observation that he longs to fly, but cannot. Nor could Robert Smith, the insurance agent overwhelmed with love, despite the mechanical contrivance of his blue silk wings:

> ...when the little boy discovered, at four, the same thing Mr Smith had learned earlier – that only birds and airplanes could fly – he lost all interest in himself. To have to live without that single gift saddened him and left his imagination so bereft that he appeared dull even to those women who did not hate his mother...
>
> (p.9)

Milkman, like Mr Smith, envisions flight only in physical terms, and therefore cannot fly without an aeroplane to help him. Only in the final moments of the novel has he learned enough from Pilate to be able to fly without wings.

Song

11.27 Language takes many forms in *Song of Solomon*, and one of the most vital is that of song. In this, too, Toni Morrison signals her awareness of the ways in which black Americans have constructed and protected their own cultural identity. Often deprived of the formal education that would have prompted them to express themselves in forms of written language, they found an equally powerful medium in music and song.

11.28 We have already given some thought to the words of the 'Song of Solomon' that gives the novel its name. One feature that we have not singled out is the fact that the song's language is not that of conventionally correct English:

> O Sugarman done fly away
> Sugarman done gone

The language of black people, sung or spoken, is distinct from that of orthodox grammar – a fact which does nothing to diminish its force. You will be able to recall other writers, from your work on Block 6, who use language deriving from traditions separate from the received norms of English grammar. Toni Morrison is at some pains to emphasize that this is not because black people are incapable of linguistic accuracy. You remember how Pilate amends Milkman's speech when she first meets him. In the opening passages of the novel, Guitar corrects the spelling of the careless white nurse who tries to send him on an errand:

> 'You left out a *s*, ma'am', the boy said. The North was new to him and he had just begun to learn he could speak up to white people. But she'd already gone, rubbing her arms against the cold.
>
> 'Granny, she left out a *s*.'
>
> 'And a "please".'
>
> (p.7)

11.29 Guitar, learning something about the shortcomings of white people from his grandmother (another of the novel's instances of a boy being taught by an older woman), also begins to acquire a sensitivity to music from her. Pilate is stirred to song by the ill-fated ambitions of Mr Smith:

> 'Who is that lady singing?'
>
> 'That, baby, is the very latest thing in pea-time.'
>
> But she smiled when she looked at the singing woman, so the cat-eyed boy listened to the musical performance with at least as much interest as he devoted to the man flapping his wings on top of the hospital.
>
> (p.8)

The brutal circumstances of Guitar's life rob him of the power of music. There is no money to buy him the guitar he longs for. Instead, he turns to hunting as the expression of his pain and his blocked desire for justice. Robert Smith, Porter and Guitar are all driven to become members of the Days, devoting themselves to the murderous pursuit of racial revenge. Like Circe, the cat-eyed Guitar – who is, again like Circe, always associated with the animal world – reduces himself to an instrument of vengeance. There is, I think (though you might well feel differently), finally an unequivocal rejection of the Days' ruthless remedies in *Song of Solomon*. Yet Guitar supports his position with some powerful arguments, and he is a figure of considerable force in the novel. Would you agree that his obsessive destructiveness is seen to be bound up with his exclusion from the song that might have given him another and more creative form of self-expression?

ACTIVITY

In thinking about feminist theories of language earlier in the block, we looked at Julia Kristeva's concept of semiotic language – a discourse distinct from what she terms the symbolic, dominated by the law. Can you think of any form of language within the novel that might correspond to Kristeva's thinking about the semiotic realm? You might find it helpful to turn back to your notes on Kristeva at this point (paragraphs 3.20–26).

DISCUSSION

You might have thought of several moments in the novel that could be approached in terms of Kristeva's ideas, and many of them are associated with both women and song. In the opening scene that we have just been thinking about, Pilate's singing is surely closer to the semiotic than the briskly callous reaction of the white people in charge of Mercy, the ironically named hospital. Macon Dead, who may be seen as the book's central representative of what Kristeva defines (after Lacan) as the symbolic order, later finds himself drawn to Pilate's singing as though to an expression of all that he has lost:

> They were singing some melody that Pilate was leading. A phrase that the other two were taking up and building on. Her powerful contralto, Reba's piercing soprano in counterpoint, and the soft voice of the girl, Hagar, who must be about ten or eleven now, pulled him like a carpet-tack under the influence of a magnet.
>
> (p.29)

But not every version of a language that could be seen as semiotic is bound up with the feminine. Hunting, too, the most masculine activity in the novel, unexpectedly reveals an order of discourse that has more to do with the semiotic than the symbolic. I wonder whether you recalled the passage in which the exhausted Milkman, sitting against a tree, hears the hunting men and dogs communicating with each other in a language which predates words:

> What were they saying? 'Wait up?' 'Over here?' Little by little it fell into place. The dogs, the men – none was just hollering, just signaling location or pace. The men and the dogs were talking to each other. In distinctive voices they were saying distinctive, complicated things. That long *yah* sound was followed by a specific kind of howl from one of the dogs. The low *howm howm* that sounded like a string bass imitating a bassoon meant something the dogs understood and executed. And the dogs spoke to the men: single-shot barks – evenly spaced and widely spaced – one every three or four minutes, that might go on for twenty minutes. A sort of radar that indicated to the men where they were and what they saw and what they wanted to do about it. And the men agreed or told them to change direction or to come back. All those shrieks, those rapid tumbling barks, the long sustained yells, the tuba sounds, the drumbeat sounds, the low liquid *howm howm*, the reedy whistles, the thin *eeeee's* of a cornet, the *unh unh unh* bass chords. It was all language. An extension of the click people made in their cheeks back home when they wanted a dog to follow them. No, it was not language; it was what there was before language. Before things were written down. Language in the time when men and animals did talk to one another, when a man could sit down with an ape and the two converse; when a tiger and a man could share the same tree, and each understood the other; when men ran *with* wolves, not from or after them.
>
> (pp.277–8)

This evocation of a primeval and almost inhuman discourse may be compared with references you have encountered in other novels in the course – in *A Passage to India*, for instance, or *Mrs Dalloway* (see Section 3). But both Forster and Woolf suggest a feminine context for such languages. Toni Morrison takes a different option. In locating her version of a language that departs from the symbolic order among men and predatory animals (the wordless humming of Circe's Weimeraners is also relevant here), as well as in women's song, she affirms Kristeva's point that the semiotic is not solely the province of the maternally nurturing feminine. Nor, as Guitar's perverted hunting instincts bear witness, is it always harmless, in a culture which denies too many of its people the right of access to a creative identity deeply rooted in the past.

11.30 Writing about a social world of mutual dependence, Toni Morrison will not allow either men or women to shelter behind the divisions of gender. The lesson of her writing is that we are already too deeply divided from each other and from ourselves, and there is too much at stake to risk any further split in a consciousness that we need to share. What *Song of Solomon* has to say about justice, power and love is directed to all of its readers – no matter what their race, sex or history. Whatever we have lost from living together, we would have more to lose from living apart.

12 Conclusion

12.1 At the beginning of Section 11, we asked whether we had arrived at a point where the association between language and gender could be charted. Now that we've come to the end of the block, have we finally reached that position? If so, what we've come up with is a guide for further journeys of exploration rather than a comprehensive map. The issues are too complicated to be summarized easily, and you may well feel that your work over the last four weeks has left you with more questions than answers.

12.2 But recognizing the questions is in itself an important advance in our understanding. Taking stock for a moment, how would you identify the most significant of the debates you have encountered as you worked through this block? I would argue that some of the most significant points are bound up with our changing sense of gender in history. Thanks to the work of feminists like Virginia Woolf, Simone de Beauvoir, Adrienne Rich – and many others, for we have had to leave a great deal out – we have been able to define new ways of looking at the historical roles of women and of men. These reconstructions of history have had crucial implications for our perceptions of literature. They have changed our view of how literature came to be written in the past, what kinds of literature have earned cultural prestige, and why – and also what kinds of literature were not written, or have remained undervalued or forgotten. And they have generated some excitingly innovative writing, of which Toni Morrison's *Song of Solomon* is a powerful example. Literature and history will be the subject of the final block of the course, which will approach this theme from a range of perspectives.

12.3 But the central focus of this block has been the relationship between language and gender, and here the arguments are as controversial as they are far-reaching. How do constructions of masculinity and femininity engage with our speech and writing? Is it possible, or desirable, to change this engagement? You have encountered the claim that women have been barred from the dominant discourses of patriarchy. If so, what can be done? Should they assert the right to enter the world of masculine language on equal terms with men? Or can they make their own kinds of language, perhaps freer and more creative than the discourses that men have made for themselves? If it is possible for women to do that, is it in their interests to perpetuate their long-established exclusion from the varieties of language which represent power in contemporary societies? The questions carry a challenge that extends far beyond the limits of the block – or indeed the course. They lie at the heart of literature in the modern world.

13 References

AIRD, E. (1973) *Sylvia Plath*, Oliver and Boyd.

ALVAREZ, A. (1963) 'Plath', *The Review*, no. 9, October.

BARBERA, J. and McBRIEN, W. (eds) (1981) *Me Again: the uncollected writings of Stevie Smith*, Virago.

BARBERA, J. and McBRIEN, W. (1985) *Stevie: a biography of Stevie Smith*, Macmillan.

DE BEAUVOIR, S. (1975) (trans. and ed. PARSHLEY, H.M. 1953), *The Second Sex*, University of North Carolina Press (first published 1949).

BELSEY, C. and MOORE, J. (eds) (1989) *The Feminist Reader: essays in gender and the politics of literary criticism*, Macmillan.

BENSON, J.J. (ed.) (1975) 'The Two African Stories' in *The Short Stories of Ernest Hemingway: critical essays*, Duke University Press.

BISHOP, E. (1984) (ed. GIROUX, R.) *The Collected Prose*, Chatto and Windus.

CHRISTIAN, B. (1985) *The Black Feminist Criticism: perspectives on black women writers*, Pergamon Press.

GAUTHIER, X. (1974) 'Oscillation between power and denial', *Tel Quel*, summer.

GREEN, M. (1974) *The Von Richthofen Sisters, The Triumphant and The Tragic Modes of Love*, University of Minnesota Press.

GURKO, L. (1968) *Ernest Hemingway: the pursuit of heroism*, Crowen Company.

HEANEY, S. (1980) *Preoccupations: selected prose 1968–1978*, Faber.

HEANEY, S. (1988) *The Government of the Tongue*, Faber.

HUGHES, T. (ed.) (1981) *Sylvia Plath: collected poems*, Faber.

JARRELL, R. (1973) *Poetry and the Age*, Faber.

JORDAN, J. (1989) *Moving Towards Home*, Virago.

LARKIN, P. (1983) *Required Writing: miscellaneous pieces 1955–1982*, Faber.

LOWELL, R. (1947) 'Thomas, Bishop and Williams', *Sewanee Review*, 55, summer.

MARKS, E. and DE COURTIVRON, I. (eds) (1981) *New French Feminisms: an anthology*, Harvester.

MILLETT, K. (1977) *Sexual Politics*, Virago (first published 1969).

MORGAN, R. (1972) 'Arraignment', *Monster*, New York.

NEWMAN, C. (ed.) (1970) *The Art of Sylvia Plath*, Faber.

ORR, P. (ed.) (1966) *The Poet Speaks*, Routledge and Kegan Paul.

PEARSALL, R.B. (1973) *The Life and Writings of Ernest Hemingway*, Amsterdam.

PLATH, S. (1965) *Ariel*, Faber.

RICH, A. (1979) *On Lies, Secrets and Silence: selected prose 1966–1978*, Norton.

RICH, A. (1980) *Snapshots of a Daughter-in-Law*, Norton (first published 1963).

RICH, A. (1984) *The Fact of a Door-Frame: poems selected and new 1950–1984*, Norton.

SELLERS, S. (ed.) (1988) *Writing Differences: readings from the seminar of Hélène Cixous*, Open University Press

SMITH, S. (1949) *The Holiday*, Chapman and Hall.

SPALDING, F. (1989) *Stevie Smith: a critical biography*, Faber.

STEINER, N.H. (1974) *A Closer Look at Ariel: a memory of Sylvia Plath*, Faber.

STEVENSON, A. (1980) 'Letters from Elizabeth Bishop', *The Times Literary Supplement*, 7 March.

THEWELEIT, K. (1987) *Male Fantasies*, Polity Press.

TRAVISANO, T.J. (1988) *Elizabeth Bishop: her artistic development*, University Press of Virginia.

WATKINS, M. (1977) 'Talk with Toni Morrison', *New York Times Book Section*, 6 September.

WILLIS, S. (1984) 'Eruptions of funk: historicizing Toni Morrison' in GATES, H.L. (ed.) *Black Literature and Literary Theory*, Methuen.

WOOLF, V. (1977) *A Room of One's Own*, Granada (first published 1929).

Acknowledgements

Grateful acknowledgement is made to the following sources for permission to reproduce material in this block: S. Plath (1960) *The Colossus*, extract from poem (p.59) reprinted by permission of Faber and Faber Ltd; T. Hughes (ed.) (1981) *Collected Poems © Sylvia Plath*, extract from poem (p.117) reprinted by permission of Faber and Faber Ltd; excerpts from 'The Fish' and 'At The Fishhouses' from *Complete Poems, 1927–1979*, by Elizabeth Bishop, copyright © 1947, 1974 by Elizabeth Bishop, copyright © 1979, 1983 by Alice Helen Methfessel, reprinted by permission of Farrar, Straus and Giroux, Inc.

BLOCK 7 LANGUAGE AND GENDER

Block 1 Introduction
Block 2 The Impact of Modernism
Block 3 'Englishness'
Block 4 Literature and Ideology
Block 5 End of Empire
Block 6 New Writings in English
Block 7 Language and Gender
Block 8 Literature and History

Cover illustration: Vanessa Bell, *Butterflies*. Woodcut reproduced from Virginia Woolf *Kew Gardens* 1919 (first edition), Hogarth Press, by permission of Angelica Garnett and Hogarth Press. British Library Cup 510 afa 3, p.16.

Photograph by permission of the British Library Board